I0132486

Professor Bloomer's AESOP'S FABLES Stimulate: Thinking, Reading Comprehension, and Morality

Adapted from a
Translation by George Fyler Townsend
Adapted by Richard H. Bloomer

Richard H Bloomer Ed.D. M.S. DABFE, FACAPP, FACFEI.
Certified Neuropsychologist
Emeritus Professor
The University of Connecticut

© Richard H Bloomer 2012

Professor Bloomer's
Aesop's Fables

A Program to Stimulate
Thinking, Reading Comprehension, and Morality

Fables as moral lessons

For centuries fables have been used to provide moral lessons, to teach the young the ways of a culture, and to transmit practical wisdom. In western culture, probably the best-known examples of this genre are the fables believed to have been written by an ancient Greek slave named Aesop. Aesop's fables encourage children to think before they act, to control impulsiveness, and to demonstrate helpfulness. They teach children to be wary of smooth talkers and other trickery. The fables also teach the value of hard work and creative thinking, and they promote self-reliance and the ability to make the best of adversity. What better subject matter to teach children to understand what they read?

Complex language and thinking

Over the last century, the American language has changed. We use shorter and less complex language than people did a hundred years ago. We use fewer words and simpler, shorter sentences. We like our language to be easily readable.

This simplification of language is especially true in public school curricula, to make learning easier for children. Unfortunately, despite this simplification, over the past century children's reading, spelling, and writing skills have declined.

Moreover, this language restriction carries a cost. Most complex thoughts require an understanding of the complex and infrequent words that we have stricken from the language of young scholars. As a result, besides decreasing young learners' skills in use of the language, we have hampered their ability to understand complex concepts. We have deprived them of the tools for using complex language and prevented their exposure to nuance and subtlety. The resulting paucity of vocabulary leads to an impoverished language and a reduced ability to think beyond the mundane.

One of the goals of Professor Bloomer's Aesop's fables, therefore, is to expose young learners to a rich vocabulary, to nuance and shading in language.

. Professor Bloomer's Aesop's fables are designed to:
   Develop higher-order thinking and reading comprehension
   Expand the student's ability to think about what he or she has read
   Relate these fables to situations in real life
   Develop moral precepts
   Expand vocabulary

Professor Bloomer's approach modifies the original Aesop's fables into a reading comprehension program by introducing the *cloze procedure* to help the reader develop focusing and comprehension skills.

Cloze procedure for enhancing understanding

The cloze procedure is a technique of deleting about 10% of words from reading materials and requiring the reader to fill in the missing words. The number of words that the reader fills in correctly can be used to determine the reading difficulty of the passage and the skill of the reader. Furthermore, since the cloze requires the reader to stop and think about what he or she is reading, it can be used to train the reader to better understand written materials.

Cloze procedure is one of the few techniques to improve reading comprehension that is supported by scientific evidence. Research shows that, when properly used, cloze actually improves not only reading comprehension and test results but also school grades.

Learners and monitors
Student selection

A student should meet two criteria before attempting Professor Bloomer's Aesop's fables:

1.   The student must be adept in reading words independently.

2.   These exercises do not teach basic reading/phonetic skills. They are designed for the student who can already read independently with little difficulty. The student who is struggling to decipher words has limited additional energy for understanding and the higher-order thought required in these exercises.

3.   The student should be beginning to able to think conceptually.

4.   Generally this developmental phase begins about age nine, grade 4, but it varies with the learner and the environment. The student who is not yet in this developmental phase will not be able to perform the tasks in these exercises and may become frustrated by them.

Note: If the student seems completely baffled by the cloze exercises, stop. Wait a year and try again. Children mature at different rates, and no good purpose is served by trying to rush their development.

Monitors

Using Professor Bloomer's Aesop's fables requires a monitor to review each lesson with the student. The monitor can be a teacher, a parent, or a tutor. In fact, any adult will do, so long as the person can read and follow the directions.

The Lessons
There are 80 cloze fables and their associated lessons in this book. Students should complete no more than two fables per week and should continue for at least forty weeks.

Each lesson will take two days. Give the students at least one day off between lessons, to allow time for their thoughts to mature and consolidate.

The lessons are not timed. The student may take as long to complete each lesson as necessary. The goal of this program is to develop student thought processes, not speed.

Day 1

Cloze (fill in the blanks)
Each cloze section includes a fable, with numbered blanks where words have been omitted, and a series of numbered spaces where the student writes the missing words.

Procedure
1. The student reads the whole fable.

2. The student writes the missing words in the blanks on the next page.

3. After filling in all the blanks for the fable, the student checks the answer key for the exact answers.

4. The student writes the number of exact answers in the space provided on the answer sheet

There are two possible types of correct answers to cloze tests:
- **Exact** answers are those written by the author and found in the answer keys in the back of the book.

- **Appropriate** answers are different from exact answers but still fit the flow of meaning in the passage. To be considered correct, these words must also be grammatically correct and spelled correctly.

1. If the answer is the exact one, it is correct.

2 If the answer is not the exact one, the monitor decides whether it is appropriate—that is, its meaning, spelling, and grammar are all correct. [Note that there may be several correct appropriate answers.]

3. If the answer is neither exact nor appropriate, the monitor may explain the correct answer to the learner.

4. The monitor writes the number of correct answers (exact answers plus appropriate answers) in the space provided.

5. The student then reads the vocabulary words and the questions for day 2, to begin preparing for the next day's session.

Day 2

Vocabulary (interesting and curious words)
Each lesson contains two or three interesting words for the student to define. Often these words are chosen for the unusual shade of meaning as used in the fable.

1. The student writes a definition of each word as it is used in the fable.

2. The student checks his or her answers in the answer sheet in the back of the book.

3. The monitor checks that the definition matches the meaning for the word in the fable. The monitor may discuss errors or other meanings of the word and how they are related to the central meaning of the word.

4. The student writes a sentence using the word.

5. The monitor checks that:
   1. The word and all other words in the sentence are spelled correctly

   2. The sentence is grammatically correct

   3. The entire sentence is written legibly

6. The monitor points out correct and incorrect interpretations and discusses the answers.

Interpretation (questions for understanding)

Each lesson contains a question or two designed to provoke thought. These questions ask the student how to interpret the fable in real life. They are designed to foster mature thought, not exact recall of the fable. In this section, there are no correct or incorrect answers to this section, only better or poorer answers.

Procedure

1.   The student writes the answers to the thought-provoking questions.

2.   The monitor determines whether the student

     a.   Understands the moral of the fable

     b.   Can apply the concept to his life

     c.   Has written the answer with correct grammar and spelling

Several levels of answer may be considered correct:

1.   **Literal**: the student repeats the message of the fable nearly word for word

2.   **Rephrasing**: the student answers using different words

3.   **Personal**: the student says something like "I would" or "I should"

4.   **Anecdotal**: the student makes up another story using different examples

5.   **Generalized A**: the student says something like "People should" and gives an example

6.   **Generalized B**: the student talks about positive and negative effects of the message

The monitor should try to lead (not push) the learner gradually to more complex thought patterns by discussing the level above the one that the student gives and by offering examples. This process may be slow, as the learners mature and gain experience.

It is important, however, that the monitor adapt to the student's level of maturity. Very young or immature children may only be able to generate literal or personal answers. are the best they can generate.   A student who is pushed too rapidly may become anxious or depressed, or may develop a low self-concept.

Maturity and thinking take time to develop. Mental maturity unfolds differently in different individuals. It depends largely on the biological maturation of the brain, but it can be encouraged by practice. The goal of this program is to encourage the development of mental maturity, by helping learners generalize their thinking and adopt a larger and larger world view.

A mentor needs patience to wait for this developmental process and the skill to perceive when the student can safely progress toward more complexity and when the student is not yet ready.

Keep in mind: There are no time limits on these exercises. The student is allowed to think as long as necessary. The goal is to develop good thinking skills, a process that takes time.

To the student: This program contains a series of lessons to help you understand better what you read and how you think about it. Each lesson will take two days.

Directions for day 1

1. On the first day of each lesson, you will receive a fable to read. But the fable has some numbered blanks where words are missing. Your job is to figure out, for each blank, a word that fits the meaning of the story.

2. On the opposite page are numbered spaces where you can write the words that correctly fill the blanks. Take your time. Find the best word for each blank, and be sure to spell your word correctly.

3. After you have finished filling in the blanks, look at the answer key in the back of the book. Mark your answer as correct if:

    a. It **exactly** matches the one in the answer key
    b. It is spelled correctly.

These are your correct **exact** answers.

4. Next, show your answers to your monitor He or she will check your answers for words that may not be the exact answers shown in the answer key but still have an **appropriate** meaning. The monitor will mark your word as correct if

    c. The meaning is appropriate
    d. The word is spelled correctly
    e. The word is grammatically correct.

These are your correct **appropriate** answers.

5. Your monitor will **determine the total number of correct answers by adding the number of correct exact** answers and the number of correct **appropriate** answers.

6. Look at the list entitled *Interesting and Curious* words for day 2. On day 2, you will be asked to define these words as they are used in the fable. You will also be

asked to write a sentence using these words. Do not write your answers now. You will have a day or two to think about your answers.

7.   Look at the section entitled **Questions for Understanding** for day 2. You will be asked to write the best answer you can think of to these questions. Use the next day or two to think about your answer.

Directions for day 2

1.   Write the definition for each of the *Interesting and Curious* words. Many words have several meanings or shades of meaning. Use the same shade of meaning that the fable uses. You may look at the fable again to help you choose the best meaning.

2.   Next, for each word, write a sentence that uses it. Try to write the best sentence you can. Take care to spell all the words in the sentence correctly.

3.   Then write the answers to the **Questions for Understanding.** Take as long as you need to write the best answer you can. If you need more space to complete your answer, use additional blank paper. You may refer back to the fable to help you answer the questions.

4.   Show your answers to your monitor. He or she will check your spelling and grammar and may discuss your answers with you.

Professor Bloomer's
AESOP'S FABLES

Cloze Exercises
to
Stimulate: Thinking, Reading
Comprehension, and Morality

Lesson 1 The Fox and the Mask

Day 1
Read the fable below. Then fill in the blanks on the next page.

A fox entered____1____ house of an actor and, rummaging through___2___ his properties, came upon a mask,___3____ admirable imitation of a human head.

He ___4___ his paws on it and said, "What___5___ beautiful head! Yet it is of no ___6___, as it entirely lacks brains."

_____

Day 2
Interesting and curious words

1.   Read the fable, and write the meaning of each word below.

   a. rummaging _____

   b. admirable _____

2.   Check your answers in the answer key on p.190. Use a dictionary to find other meanings

   for the words.

.

3.   Below, write a sentence using each word as it is used in the fable.

   a. _____

   _____

   b. _____

   _____

Lesson 1 The Fox and the Mask

Day 1

Fill in the blanks Write your answers below

1. _____   4. _____

2. _____   5. _____

3. _____   6. _____

Correct exact words   _____

Correct appropriate words   _____

Total correct words   _____

Day 2

Questions for understanding: Write your answers below.

1. In this fable, how would you describe the fox?

_____

_____

_____

_____

2. What is the main theme of this fable?

_____

_____

_____

_____

Lesson 2 The Fox and the Grapes

Day 1
Read the fable below. Then fill in the blanks on the next page.

A famished fox saw some clusters of ____1____ black grapes hanging from a trellised vine. ____2____ resorted to all her tricks to get at ___3___, but tired herself in vain. She could ____4____ reach the grapes.

At last she turned ____5____, hiding her disappointment and saying, "Those grapes ____6____ sour and not ripe as I thought."

_____

Day 2
Interesting and curious words

1. Read the fable, and write the meaning of each word below.

    a. famished _____

    b. trellised _____

    c. vain _____

2. Check your answers in the key on p. 190. Use a dictionary to find other meanings for the
    words.

3.   Below, write a sentence using each word as it is used in the fable.
    a. _____

    _____

    b. _____

    _____

    c. _____

    _____

Lesson 2 The Fox and the Grapes

Day 1

Fill in the blanks Write your answers below

1. _____   4. _____

2. _____   5. _____

3. _____   6. _____

Correct exact words   _____

Correct appropriate words   _____

Total correct words   _____

Day 2

Questions for understanding: Write your answers below.

1. How is the fox in this fable different from the fox in the first fable?

_____

_____

_____

_____

2. What is the main theme of this fable?

_____

_____

_____

_____

Lesson 3 The Fox and the Leopard

Day 1
Read the fable below. Then fill in the blanks on the next page.

The fox and the leopard argued ____1____ which was the more beautiful of the
____2____. The leopard exhibited one by one the ___3___ spots that decorated his skin.

But the ___4___, interrupting him, said, "And how much ___5___ beautiful than you am I,
who ___6___ decorated, not in body, but in mind."

____7____ is more than skin deep.

_____

Day 2
Interesting and curious words

1.   Read the fable, and write the meaning of each word below.

   a. exhibited _____

   b. decorated _____

2.   Check your answers using the answer key on p. 190. Use a dictionary to find other
        meanings for the words.
   .   Below, write a sentence using each word as it is used in the fable.

   a. _____

   _____

   b. _____

   _____

Lesson 3 The Fox and the Leopard

Day 1

Fill in the blanks. Write your answers below.

1. _____

2. _____

3. _____

4. _____

5. _____

6. _____

7. _____

Correct exact words   _____

Correct appropriate words   _____

Total correct words   _____

Day 2

Questions for understanding: Write your answers below: Write your answers below.

1. What kind of person is the leopard?

_____

_____

_____

_____

2. What does the fox mean when he says, "I am decorated in mind"?

_____

_____

_____

_____

Lesson 4 The Boy Bathing

Day 1
Read the fable below. Then fill in the blanks on the next page.

A boy bathing ____1____ a river was in danger of being drowned. ____2____ called out to a
       passing traveler for ____3____. But instead of holding out a helping ____4____, the man
       stood by unconcernedly and scolded ____5____ boy for his imprudence.

"Oh, sir!" cried ____6____ youth, "pray help me now and scold ____7____ afterwards."

Counsel without help is useless.

_____

Day 2
Interesting and curious words

1.   Read the fable, and write the meaning of each word below.

   a. unconcernedly _____

   b. scold_____

   c. imprudence_____

2.   Check your answers using the answer key on p. 190. Use a dictionary to find other
        meanings for the words.

3.   Below, write a sentence using each word as it is used in the fable.

   a. _____

   _____

   b. _____

   _____

   c. _____

   _____

Lesson 4 The Boy Bathing

Day 1

Fill in the blanks. Write your answers below.

1. _____   5. _____

2. _____   6. _____

3. _____   7. _____

4. _____

Correct exact words   _____
Correct appropriate words   _____
Total correct words   _____

Day 2

Questions for understanding: Write your answers below.

1. What is the man in this fable like?

_____

_____

_____

_____

2. What would you do if you saw a boy in the river?

_____

_____

_____

_____

Lesson 5 The Rabbit and the Hound

Day 1
Read the fable below. Then fill in the blanks on the next page.

A hound started a ___1___ from his lair, but after a long run, ___2___ up the chase. A goatherd, seeing ___3___ stop, mocked him, saying, "The little rabbit ___4___ the better runner of the two."

The ___5___ replied, "You do not see the difference ___6___ us: I was only running for a ___7___, but he was running for his life."

_____

—

Day 2
Interesting and curious words

1.   Read the fable, and write the meaning of each word below.

a. lair_____

b. mocked_____

2.   Check your answers using the answer key on p. 190. Use a dictionary to find other meanings for the words.

3.   Below, write a sentence using each word as it is used in the fable.

a. _____

_____

b. _____

_____

Lesson 5 The Rabbit and the Hound

Day 1
Fill in the blanks. Write your answers below.

1. _____   5. _____

2. _____   6. _____

3. _____   7. _____

4. _____

Correct exact words   _____
Correct appropriate words   _____
Total correct words   _____

Day 2
Questions for understanding: Write your answers below.

1. Why did the rabbit beat the dog?

_____

_____

_____

_____

2. What does this fable tell you about motivation?

_____

_____

_____

_____

Lesson 6 The Dog in the Manger

Day 1
Read the fable below. Then fill in the blanks on the next page.

A dog lay ___1___ a manger. He growled and snapped every ___2___ the oxen came near.
He prevented the ___3___ from eating the hay that had been ___4___ for them.

"What a selfish dog!" said ___5___ of them to his companions. "He cannot
___6___ the hay himself and yet refuses to ___7___ those to eat who can."

Selfish greed ___8___ no one.

_____

Day 2
Interesting and curious words

1.   Read the fable, and write the meaning of each word below.

   a. prevented_____

   b. manger_____

2.   Check your answers using the answer key on p. 190. Use a dictionary to find other
       meanings for the words.

3.   Below, write a sentence using each word as it is used in the fable.

   a. _____

   _____

   b. _____

   _____

Lesson 6 The Dog in the Manger

Day 1
Fill in the blanks. Write your answers below.

1. _____

2. _____

3. _____

4. _____

5. _____

6. _____

7. _____

8. _____

Correct exact words   _____

Correct appropriate words   _____

Total correct words   _____

Day 2
Questions for understanding: Write your answers below.

1. Why do you think the dog snapped at the oxen?

_____

_____

_____

_____

2. In this fable, who was the winner?

_____

_____

_____

_____

Lesson 7 The Donkey and His Driver

Day 1
Read the fable below. Then fill in the blanks on the next page.

A donkey, being ___1___ along a high road, suddenly started off ___2___ bolted
to the brink of a ___3___ precipice. While he was in the act ___4___ throwing himself over, his
owner seized him ___5___ the tail, endeavoring to pull him back.

___6___ the donkey persisted in his effort, the ___7___ let him go and said, "Follow
your ___8___ ideas but be prepared for the cost."

Day 2
Interesting and curious words

1. Read the fable, and write the meaning of each word below.

   a. bolted_____

   b. precipice _____

   c. endeavoring_____

2. Check your answers using the answer key on p. 190. Use a dictionary to find other
    meanings for the words.

3. Below, write a sentence using each word as it is used in the fable.

   a. _____

   _____

   b. _____

   _____

   c. _____

   _____

Lesson 7 The Donkey and His Driver

Day 1
Fill in the blanks. Write your answers below.

1. _____   5. _____

2. _____   6. _____

3. _____   7. _____

4. _____   8. _____

Correct exact words   _____
Correct appropriate words   _____
Total correct words   _____

Day 2
Questions for understanding: Write your answers below.

1. What do you think the donkey is like?

_____

_____

_____

_____

2. What would it be like if everyone acted like the donkey?

_____

_____

_____

_____

Lesson 8 The Hawk, the Eagle, and the Pigeons

Day 1
Read the fable below. Then fill in the blanks on the next page.

Some pigeons, terrified ____1____ an eagle circling in the sky overhead, ____2____ upon a hawk to defend them. He ____3____ once consented.

When the pigeons let the hawk ____4____ the pigeon cote, they found that he ____5____ more havoc and slew a larger number ____6____ them in one day than the eagle ____7____ have captured in a whole year.

Avoid ____8____ remedy that is worse than the disease.

Day 2
Interesting and curious words

1. Read the fable, and write the meaning of each word below.

   a. cote_____

   b. consented_____

   c. havoc_____

2. Check your answers using the answer key on p. 190. Use a dictionary to find other meanings for the words.

3. Below, write a sentence using each word as it is used in the fable.

   a._____

   _____

   b. _____

   _____

   c. _____

   _____

Lesson 8 The Hawk, the Eagle, and the Pigeons

Day 1
Fill in the blanks. Write your answers below.

1. _____

2. _____

3. _____

4. _____

5. _____

6. _____

7. _____

8. _____

Correct exact words   _____
Correct appropriate words   _____
Total correct words   _____

Day 2
Questions for understanding: Write your answers below.

1. What mistake did the pigeons make?

_____

_____

_____

_____

2. Can you think of a time when people acted like the pigeons?

_____

_____

_____

_____

Lesson 9The Wolf and the Lion

Day 1
Read the fable below. Then fill in the blanks on the next page.

A wolf, having stolen a lamb from ___1___ fold, was carrying him off to his ___2___.
A lion met him in the path ___3___, seizing the lamb, took it from him.

___4___ at a safe distance, the wolf exclaimed, "___5___ have unrighteously taken that which was mine!"

___6___ which the lion jeeringly replied, "It was ___7___ yours, eh? The gift of a friend?"

_____

Day 2
Interesting and curious words

1.   Read the fable, and write the meaning of each word below.

   a. seizing _____

   b. jeer_____

   c. righteous_____

2.   Check your answers in the answer key on p.190. Use a dictionary to find other meanings
        for the words.

3.   Below, write a sentence using each word as it is used in the fable.

   a._____

   _____

   b. _____

   _____

   c. _____

   _____

Lesson 9The Wolf and the Lion

Day 1
Fill in the blanks. Write your answers below.

1. _____

2. _____

3. _____

4. _____

5. _____

6. _____

7. _____

Correct exact words   _____
Correct appropriate words   _____
Total correct words   _____

Day 2
Questions for understanding: Write your answers below.

1. In this fable, who do you think did the right thing?

_____

_____

_____

_____

2. What is the main idea of this fable?

_____

_____

_____

_____

Lesson 10 The Thrush and the Fowler

Day 1
Read the fable below. Then fill in the blanks on the next page.

A thrush ___1___ feeding on a myrtle tree and did ___2___ move from it because its berries were ___3___ delicious. A fowler observed her staying so ___4___ in one spot, and cast his net ___5___ caught her.

The thrush, being at the ___6___ of death, exclaimed, "O foolish creature that ___7___ am! For the sake of a little ___8___ food I have deprived myself of my ___9___."

_____

Day 2
Interesting and curious words

1.   Read the fable, and write the meaning of each word below.

   a. cast _____

   b. deprived_____

   c. fowler _____

2.   Check your answers in the answer key on p.190. Use a dictionary to find other meanings for the words.

3.   Below, write a sentence using each word as it is used in the fable.

   a._____

   _____

   b. _____

   _____

   c. _____

   _____

Lesson 10 The Thrush and the Fowler

Day 1
Fill in the blanks. Write your answers below.

1. _____   6. _____

2. _____   7. _____

3. _____   8. _____

4. _____   9. _____

5. _____

Correct exact words   _____
Correct appropriate words   _____
Total correct words   _____

Day 2
Questions for understanding: Write your answers below.

1. Can you think of anything that would have saved the thrush?

_____

_____

_____

_____

2. What is this fable trying to tell you?

_____

_____

_____

_____

Lesson 11 The Dog and the Oyster

Day 1
Read the fable below. Then fill in the blanks on the next page.

A dog, used ____1____ eating eggs, saw an oyster and, opening ____2____ mouth to its widest extent, swallowed it ____3____ with the utmost relish, supposing it to ____4____ an egg.

Soon afterwards, suffering great pain ____5____ his stomach, he said, "I deserve all ____6____ torment, for my folly in thinking that ____7____ round must be an egg."

They who act without sufficient thought will ____8____ fall into unsuspected danger.

_____

Day 2
Interesting and curious words

1.   Read the fable, and write the meaning of each word below.

   a. folly_____

   b. utmost _____

   c. relish _____

2.   Check your answers in the answer key on p.190. Use a dictionary to find other meanings
      for the words.

3.   Below, write a sentence using each word as it is used in the fable.

   a. _____

   _____

   b. _____

   _____

   c. _____

   _____

Lesson 11 The Dog and the Oyster

Day 1
Fill in the blanks. Write your answers below.

1. _____   5. _____

2. _____   6. _____

3. _____   7. _____

4. _____   8. _____

Correct exact words   _____
Correct appropriate words   _____
Total correct words   _____

Day 2
Questions for understanding: Write your answers below.

1. How could the dog have saved himself from the pain?

_____

_____

_____

_____

2. What does this fable tell you about things that look alike?

_____

_____

_____

_____

Lesson 12 The Wolf, the Fox, and the Ape

Day 1
Read the fable below. Then fill in the blanks on the next page.

A wolf accused a ___1___ of theft, but the fox entirely denied ___2___ charge. An ape
undertook to judge the matter ___3___ them.

When each had fully stated his ___4___, the ape announced this sentence: "I do _
___5___ think you, Wolf, ever lost what you ___6___; and I do believe you, Fox, to
have ___7___ what you so stoutly deny."

The dishonest, ___8___ they act honestly, get no credit.

_____

Day 2
Interesting and curious words

1.   Read the fable, and write the meaning of each word below.

  a. adjudge_____

  b. stoutly_____

  c. undertook _____

2.   Check your answers in the answer key on p.190. Use a dictionary to find other meanings
      for the words.

3.   Below, write a sentence using each word as it is used in the fable.

  a. _____

  _____

  b. _____

  _____

  c. _____

  _____

Lesson 12 The Wolf, the Fox, and the Ape

Day 1

Fill in the blanks. Write your answers below.

1. _____   5. _____

2. _____   6. _____

3. _____   7. _____

4. _____   8. _____

Correct exact words   _____

Correct appropriate words   _____

Total correct words   _____

Day 2

Questions for understanding: Write your answers below.

1. What evidence was the ape using to make his judgment?

_____

_____

_____

_____

2. What does this fable tell you about a person's reputation?

_____

_____

_____

_____

Lesson 13 The Partridge and the Fowler

Day 1
Read the fable below. Then fill in the blanks on the next page.

A fowler ___1___ a partridge and was about to kill ___2___. The partridge earnestly beseeched the fowler to spare ___3___ life, saying, "Pray, master, permit me to ___4___ and I will entice many partridges to ___5___ in recompense for your mercy to me."

___6___ fowler replied, "I shall now take your ___7___ with less scruple, because you are willing ___8___ save it at the cost of betraying ___9___ friends and relations."

_____

Day 2
Interesting and curious words

1.   Read the fable, and write the meaning of each word below.

a. beseeched_____

b. enticed_____

c. scruple_____

2.   Check your answers in the answer key on p.191. Use a dictionary to find other meanings for the words.

3.   Below, write a sentence using each word as it is used in the fable.

a. _____

_____

b. _____

_____

c. _____

_____

Lesson 13 The Partridge and the Fowler

Day 1
Fill in the blanks. Write your answers below.

Fill in the blanks Write your answers below

1. _____   6. _____

2. _____   7. _____

3. _____   8. _____

4. _____   9. _____

5. _____

Correct exact words   _____

Correct appropriate words   _____

Total correct words   _____

Day 2
Questions for understanding: Write your answers below.

1. What kind of person was the partridge?

_____

_____

_____

_____

2. Why didn't the fowler accept the partridge's help?

_____

_____

_____

_____

Lesson 14 The Dolphins, the Whales, and the Herring

Day 1
Read the fable below. Then fill in the blanks on the next page.

The dolphins and whales ____1____ a fierce war with each other. When ____2____ battle was at its height, a herring ____3____ its head out of the waves and ____4____ that he would settle their differences if ____5____ would accept him as an umpire.

One ____6____ the dolphins replied, "We would far rather ____7____ destroyed in our battle with each other ____8____ accept any interference from a lowly herring ____9____ our affairs."

Day 2
Interesting and curious words

1.   Read the fable, and write the meaning of each word below.

a. umpire_____

b. affairs_____

2. Check your answers in the answer key on p.191. Use a dictionary to find other meanings for the words.

3. Below, write a sentence using each word as it is used in the fable.

a. _____

_____

b. _____

_____

Lesson 14 The Dolphins, the Whales, and the Herring

Day 1
Fill in the blanks. Write your answers below

1. _____   6. _____

2. _____   7. _____

3. _____   8. _____

4. _____   9. _____

5. _____

Correct exact words   _____

Correct appropriate words   _____

Total correct words   _____

Day 2
Questions for understanding: Write your answers below.

1. Why did the whales and dolphins reject the herring's help?

_____

_____

_____

_____

2. What might have happened if the herring had tried to settle the differences?

_____

_____

_____

_____

Lesson 15 The Dog's House

Day 1
Read the fable below. Then fill in the blanks on the next page.

In _____1_____ wintertime, a dog curled up in as _____2_____ a space as possible. He was so
_____3_____ that he determined to make himself a house.

_____4_____, when the summer returned, he lay _____5_____
stretched at his full length and appeared _____6_____ himself to be of a great size. _____7_____ he
considered that it would be neither _____8_____ easy nor a necessary task to make _____9_____ such
a house as would accommodate him.

_____

Day 2
Interesting and curious words

1.   Read the fable, and write the meaning of each word below.

   a. determined _____

   b. accommodate_____

2.   Check your answers in the answer key on p.191. Use a dictionary to find other meanings
       for the words.

3.   Below, write a sentence using each word as it is used in the fable.

   a. _____

   _____

   b. _____

   _____

Lesson 15 The Dog's House

Day 1
Fill in the blanks. Write your answers below.

1. _____   6. _____

2. _____   7. _____

3. _____   8. _____

4. _____   9. _____

5. _____

Correct exact words   _____
Correct appropriate words   _____
Total correct words   _____

Lesson 15

Day 2
Questions for understanding: Write your answers below.

1. What kind of person is the dog?

_____

_____

_____

_____

2. What do you think will happen next winter?

_____

_____

_____

_____

Lesson 16 The Cock and the Jewel

Day 1
Read the fable below. Then fill in the blanks on the next page.

A rooster ____1____ scratching in the barnyard for food for ____2____ and his hens. He found a precious ___3___.

The rooster exclaimed, "If my owner had ____4____ this jewel, and not I, he would ____5____ rich and live in a big house. ____6____ hens and I have no use for ____7____. I would rather have one ear of ____8____ than all the jewels in the world

____9____ *according to his needs.*

_____

Day 2
Interesting and curious words

1.   Read the fable, and write the meaning of each word below.

   a. precious_____

   b. exclaimed_____

2.   Check your answers in the answer key on p.191. Use a dictionary to find other meanings for the words.

3.   Below, write a sentence using each word as it is used in the fable.

   a. _____

   _____

   b. _____

   _____

Lesson 16 The Cock and the Jewel

Day 1
Fill in the blanks. Write your answers below.

1. _____   6. _____

2. _____   7. _____

3. _____   8. _____

4. _____   9. _____

5. _____

Correct exact words   _____

Correct appropriate words   _____

Total correct words   _____

Day 2
Questions for understanding: Write your answers below.

1. Why did the rooster leave the jewel in the barnyard?

_____

_____

_____

_____

2. What does this fable say about things of value?

_____

_____

_____

_____

Lesson 17 The Flies and the Honey Pot

Day 1
Read the fable below. Then fill in the blanks on the next page.

A number of flies ____1____ attracted to a jar of honey that ____2____ been overturned in a kitchen, and they crowded ____3____ to eat greedily. However, they became so ____4____ with the honey that they could not ____5____ their feet or wings, nor release themselves, ____6____ were suffocated.

Just as they were expiring, ____7____ exclaimed, "O foolish creatures that we are. For ____8____ sake of a little pleasure, we have ____9____ ourselves."

Pleasure that brings pain hurts

.

_____

Day 2
Interesting and curious words

1.   Read the fable, and write the meaning of each word below.
a. greedily_____

b. smeared_____

c. expiring_____

2.   Check your answers in the answer key on p.191. Use a dictionary to find other meanings for the words.

   3.   Below, write a sentence using each word as it is used in the fable.

   a. _____

   _____

   b. _____

   _____

   c. _____

   _____

Lesson 17 The Flies and the Honey Pot

Day 1
Fill in the blanks. Write your answers below.

1. _____

2. _____

3. _____

4. _____

5. _____

6. _____

7. _____

8. _____

9. _____

Correct exact words _____

Correct appropriate words _____

Total correct words _____

Day 2
Questions for understanding: Write your answers below.

1. What does this fable say about having all the sweets you want?

_____

_____

_____

_____

2. What does this fable tell you about greedy people?

_____

_____

_____

_____

Lesson 18 The Gnat and the Bull

Day 1
Read the fable below. Then fill in the blanks on the next page.

A gnat settled ____1____ the horn of a bull and sat ____2____ a long time. Just as he was ____3____ to fly off, he made a buzzing ____4____, and inquired of the bull if he ____5____ like him to go.

The bull replied, "____6____ did not know you had come, and I ____7____ not miss you when you go away."

Some ____8____ of more importance in their own eyes ____9____ in the eyes of their neighbors.

_____

Day 2
Interesting and curious words

1.   Read the fable, and write the meaning of each word below.

  a. inquired _____

  b. gnat_____

2.   Check your answers in the answer key on p.191. Use a dictionary to find other meanings for the words.

3.   Below, write a sentence using each word as it is used in the fable.

  a. _____

  _____

  b. _____

  _____

Lesson 18 The Gnat and the Bull

Day 1
Fill in the blanks. Write your answers below.

1. _____   6. _____

2. _____   7. _____

3. _____   8. _____

4. _____   9. _____

5. _____

Correct exact words   _____
Correct appropriate words   _____
Total correct words   _____

Day 2
Questions for understanding: Write your answers below.

1. Why did the gnat tell the bull that he was leaving?

_____

_____

_____

_____

2. What is this fable trying to tell you?

_____

_____

_____

_____

Lesson 19 The Mother Dog and Her Whelps

Day 1
Read the fable below. Then fill in the blanks on the next page.

A mother dog, ____1____ to whelp, earnestly begged a shepherd for ____2____ place where she might have her litter.

____3____ her request was granted, she sought permission ____4____ rear her puppies in the same spot. ____5____ shepherd again consented.

At last, the ____6____ dog, protected by the bodyguard of her ____7____, who had now grown up and were ____8____ to defend themselves, asserted her exclusive right ____9____ the place and would not permit the ____10____ to approach.

_____

Day 2
Interesting and curious words

1.   Read the fable, and write the meaning of each word below.

   a. whelp _____

   b. litter_____

2.   Check your answers in the answer key on p.191. Use a dictionary to find other meanings ·
        for the words.

3.   Below, write a sentence using each word as it is used in the fable.

   a. _____

   _____

   b. _____

   _____

Lesson 19 The Mother Dog and Her Whelps

Day 1
Fill in the blanks. Write your answers below.

1. _____   6. _____

2. _____   7. _____

3. _____   8. _____

4. _____   9. _____

5. _____   10. _____

Correct exact words   _____
Correct appropriate words   _____
Total correct words   _____

Day 2
Questions for understanding: Write your answers below.

1. Why did the mother dog and her whelps protect the spot they were born?

_____

_____

_____

_____

2. What is this fable trying to tell you?

_____

_____

_____

_____

Lesson 20 The Fox and the Lion

Day 1
Read the fable below. Then fill in the blanks on the next page.

A fox, ____1____ had never yet seen a lion, saw ____2____ by chance for the first time in
____3____ forest. The fox was so frightened that he ____4____ died with fear.

On meeting the lion for ____5____ second time, the fox was still much alarmed, ____6____ not to
the same extent as at ____7____ .

On seeing the lion the third time, the fox ____8____ so increased in boldness that he went
____9____ to him and commenced a familiar conversation ____10____ him.

Acquaintance softens prejudices.

_____

Day 2
Interesting and curious words

Read the fable, and write the meaning of each word below.

a. alarmed_____

b. commenced_____

Check your answers in the answer key on p.191. Use a dictionary to find other meanings for the
words.

· Below, write a sentence using each word as it is used in the fable.

a. _____

_____

b. _____

_____

c. _____

_____

Lesson 20 The Fox and the Lion

Day 1
Fill in the blanks. Write your answers below.

1. _____   6. _____

2. _____   7. _____

3. _____   8. _____

4. _____   9. _____

5. _____   10. _____

Correct exact words   _____
Correct appropriate words   _____
Total correct words   _____

Day 2
Questions for understanding: Write your answers below.

1. Why did the fox begin to talk to the lion?

_____

_____

_____

_____

2. What does this fable teach you about fear?

_____

_____

_____

_____

Lesson 21 The Flea and the Man

Day 1
Read the fable below. Then fill in the blanks on the next page.

A man, very much annoyed _____1_____ a flea, caught him at last, and _____2_____ him, "Who are you who dare to feed _____3_____ my limbs, and to cost me so _____4_____ trouble in catching you?"

The flea replied, "_____5_____, dear sir, spare my life. Do not _____6_____ me, for I cannot possibly do you _____7_____ harm."

The man, laughing, replied, "Now you _____8_____ certainly die by my own hand, for _____9_____ evil, whether it be small or large, _____10_____ be tolerated."

_____

Day 2
Interesting and curious words

1.   Read the fable, and write the meaning of each word below.

   a. annoyed_____

   b. tolerated_____

2.   Check your answers in the answer key on p.191. Use a dictionary to find other meanings for the words.

3.   Below, write a sentence using each word as it is used in the fable.

      a. _____

      _____

      b. _____

      _____

Lesson 21 The Flea and the Man

Fill in the blanks. Write your answers below.

1. _____

2. _____

3. _____

4. _____

5. _____

6. _____

7. _____

8. _____

9. _____

10. _____

Correct exact words   _____

Correct appropriate words _____

Total correct words   _____

Day 2
Questions for understanding: Write your answers below.

1. What would you do if you caught a flea?

_____

_____

_____

_____

2. What lesson can you learn from this fable?

_____

_____

_____

_____

Lesson 22 The Donkey and the Charger

Day 1
Read the fable below. Then fill in the blanks on the next page.

A donkey was jealous ____1____ a charger who was carefully ____2____ ungrudgingly taken care of. The donkey himself ____3____ to work hard and had scarcely enough ____4____ eat.

But when war broke out, a ____5____ armed soldier mounted the charger and, riding ____6____ to the battle, rushed into the very midst ____7____ the enemy. The charger was wounded and fell ____8____ on the battlefield. The donkey, seeing all ____9____ things, changed his mind, and commiserated with the ____10____.

_____

Day 2
Interesting and curious words

1.   Read the fable, and write the meaning of each word below.

   a. charger_____

   b. ungrudgingly_____

   c. commiserate_____

2.   Check your answers in the answer key on p.191. Use a dictionary to find other meanings for the words.

3.   Below, write a sentence using each word as it is used in the fable.

   a. _____

   _____

   b. _____

   _____

   c. _____

   _____

Lesson 22 The Donkey and the Charger

Day 1
Fill in the blanks. Write your answers below.

1. _____   6. _____

2. _____   7. _____

3. _____   8. _____

4. _____   9. _____

5. _____   10. _____

Correct exact words   _____

Correct appropriate words _____

Total correct words   _____

Day 2
Questions for understanding: Write your answers below.

1. Why was the donkey jealous?

_____

_____

_____

_____

2. What does this fable teach you about understanding others?

_____

_____

_____

_____

Lesson 23 The Camel

Day 1
Read the fable below. Then fill in the blanks on the next page.

When a man first ____1____ a camel looming in the desert, he ____2____ so frightened at the animal's vast size that ____3____ ran away.

After a time watching the ____4____ from a distance, the man perceived the meekness ____5____ gentleness of the beast's temper. The man summoned ____6____ enough to approach the camel.

Soon after, ____7____ that the camel was altogether docile, the man ____8____ bold enough to put a bridle in ____9____ mouth, and to let a child drive ____10____.

Familiarity serves to overcome dread.

_____

Day 2
Interesting and curious words

1.   Read the fable, and write the meaning of each word below.

 a. looming_____

 b. vast_____

 c. meekness_____

2.   Check your answers in the answer key on p.191. Use a dictionary to find other meanings for the words.

3.   Below, write a sentence using each word as it is used in the fable.

 a. _____

 _____

 b. _____

 _____

 c. _____

 _____

Lesson 23 The Camel

Day 1
Fill in the blanks. Write your answers below.

1. _____   6. _____

2. _____   7. _____

3. _____   8. _____

4. _____   9. _____

5. _____   10. _____

Correct exact words   _____
Correct appropriate words   _____
Total correct words   _____

Day 2
Questions for understanding: Write your answers below.

1. Why did the camel let the man put a bridle on him?

_____

_____

_____

_____

2. What lesson can you learn about fear from this fable?

_____

_____

_____

_____

Lesson 24 The Monkeys and Their Mother

Day 1
Read the fable below. Then fill in the blanks on the next page.

The mother monkey, it ____1____ said, often has two young ones at ____2____ birth. The mother fondles one and nurtures ____3____ with the greatest affection and care, but ____4____ mother often dislikes and neglects the other.

____5____ happens that the young one who is caressed and ____6____ is smothered by the too great affection ____7____ the mother. He becomes lazy and requires ____8____ mother to bring him food. The despised ____9____, who was nurtured and reared in neglect, ____10____ goes on to great success.

The best intentions will not always ensure success.

Day 2
Interesting and curious words

1.   Read the fable, and write the meaning of each word below.

a. smothered _____

b. nurtured _____

2.   Check your answers in the answer key on p.191. Use a dictionary to find other meanings for the words.

3.   Below, write a sentence using each word as it is used in the fable

a. _____

_____

b. _____

_____

Lesson 24 The Monkeys and Their Mother

Day 1
Fill in the blanks. Write your answers below.

1. _____   6. _____

2. _____   7. _____

3. _____   8. _____

4. _____   9. _____

5. _____   10. _____

Correct exact words   _____
Correct appropriate words   _____
Total correct words   _____

Day 2
Questions for understanding: Write your answers below.

1. What does this fable teach you about raising the young?

_____

_____

_____

_____

2. Why was the second monkey a success?

_____

_____

_____

_____

Lesson 25 The Boy and the Filberts

Day 1
Read the fable below. Then fill in the blanks on the next page.

A boy put his _____1_____ into a pitcher full of filberts. He _____2_____ as many
as he could possibly hold, _____3_____ when he tried to pull out his _____4_____, he
was prevented from doing so by _____5_____ neck of the pitcher.

Unwilling to lose _____6_____ filberts, and yet unable to withdraw his _____7_____, he burst into
tears and bitterly lamented _____8_____ disappointment.

A bystander said to him, "Be _____9_____ with half the quantity, and you will _____10_____ withdraw
your hand."

_____

Day 2
Interesting and curious words

1.   Read the fable, and write the meaning of each word below.

   a. bystander _____

   b. bitterly_____

   c. lamented_____

   2. Check your answers in the answer key on p.192. Use a dictionary to find other meanings for
   the words.

   3. Below, write a sentence using each word as it is used in the fable.

   a. _____

   _____

   b. _____

   _____

   c. _____

   _____

Lesson 25 The Boy and the Filberts

Day 1
Fill in the blanks. Write your answers below.

1. _____   6. _____

2. _____   7. _____

3. _____   8. _____

4. _____   9. _____

5. _____   10. _____

Correct exact words   _____

Correct appropriate words   _____

Total correct words   _____

Day 2
Questions for understanding: Write your answers below.

1. Why did the boy get his hand stuck?

_____

_____

_____

_____

2. What does this fable tell you about learning new things?

_____

_____

_____

_____

Lesson 26 The Peacock and the Crane

Day 1
Read the fable below. Then fill in the blanks on the next page.

A peacock, spreading ____1____ gorgeous tail, mocked a crane that passed ____2____, ridiculing the plain color of its plumage by ____3____ : "I am dressed like a king, in ____4____ and purple and all the colors of ____5____ rainbow, while you do not have a ____6____ of color on your wings."

"True," replied the ____7____, "but I soar to the heights of ____8____ and lift up my voice to the ____9____, while you can only walk below, like ____10____ rooster, among the birds of the barnyard."

____11____ feathers do not make fine birds.

_____

Day 2
Interesting and curious words

1.   Read the fable, and write the meaning of each word below.

 a. gorgeous _____

 b. ridiculing _____

 c. soar _____

2.   Check your answers in the answer key on p.192. Use a dictionary to find other meanings
         for the words.

3.   Below, write a sentence using each word as it is used in the fable.

 a._____

 _____

 b. _____

 _____

 c. _____

 _____

60

Lesson 26 The Peacock and the Crane

Day 1
Fill in the blanks. Write your answers below.

1. _____   7. _____

2. _____   8. _____

3. _____   9. _____

4. _____   10. _____

5. _____   11. _____

6. _____

Correct exact words   _____

Correct appropriate words   _____

Total correct words   _____

Day 2
Questions for understanding: Write your answers below.

1. What kind of person is the peacock?

_____

_____

_____

_____

2. What does this fable tell you about beautiful clothes?

_____

_____

_____

_____

Lesson 27 The Wolf and the Lion

Day 1
Read the fable below. Then fill in the blanks on the next page.

Roaming by the mountainside ____1____ sundown, a wolf saw his own shadow ____2____ greatly extended and magnified, and he said ____3____ himself, "Look at how huge I am. ____4____ am so immense that I extend nearly an ____5____ in length. Why should I be afraid ____6____ the lion? Shouldn't I be acknowledged as king ____7____ all the collected beasts?"

While he was ____8____ in these proud thoughts, a lion fell ____9____ him and killed him.
The wolf exclaimed with ____10____ too-late repentance
: "Wretched me! This overestimation ____11____ myself is the cause of my destruction."

_____

Day 2
Interesting and curious words

1.   Read the fable, and write the meaning of each word below.

  a. wretched _____

  b. immense _____

  c. repentance _____

2.   Check your answers in the answer key on p.192. Use a dictionary to find other meanings for the words.

3.   Below, write a sentence using each word as it is used in the fable.

  a. _____

  _____

  b. _____

  _____

  c. _____

  _____

62

Lesson 27 The Wolf and the Lion

Day 1
Fill in the blanks. Write your answers below.

1. _____

2. _____

3. _____

4. _____

5. _____

6. _____

7. _____

8. _____

9. _____

10. _____

11. _____

Correct exact words   _____

Correct appropriate words   _____

Total correct words   _____

Day 2
Questions for understanding: Write your answers below.

1. What did the wolf do to get himself killed?

_____

_____

_____

_____

2. What is this fable trying to tell you?

_____

_____

_____

_____

Lesson 28 The Wolf and the Horse

Day 1
Read the fable below. Then fill in the blanks on the next page.

A wolf ____1____ out of a field of oats met ____2____ horse and thus addressed him:
"I would ____3____ you to go into that field. It ____4____ full of fine oats. Since you are
____5____ good friend, I have left them untouched ____6____ you. I would love to hear you
enjoying ____7____ them."

The horse replied, "If oats were ____8____ food of wolves, you would never have indulged
____9____ ears at the cost of your belly."

____10____ of evil reputation, when they perform a ____11____ deed, fail to get credit for it.

_____

Day 2
Interesting and curious words

1.   Read the fable, and write the meaning of each word below.

   a. addressed _____

   b. advised _____

   c. indulged _____

2.   Check your answers in the answer key on p.192. Use a dictionary to find other meanings
      for the words.

3.   Below, write a sentence using each word as it is used in the fable.

   a. _____

   _____

   b. _____

   _____

   c. _____

   _____

Lesson 28 The Wolf and the Horse

Day 1
Fill in the blanks. Write your answers below.

1. _____

2. _____

3. _____

4. _____

5. _____

6. _____

7. _____

8. _____

9. _____

10. _____

11. _____

Correct exact words   _____
Correct appropriate words   _____
Total correct words   _____

Day 2
Questions for understanding: Write your answers below.

1. Why was the wolf so generous with the oats?

_____

_____

_____

_____

2. What would you think of someone who acts like the wolf in this fable?

_____

_____

_____

_____

Lesson 29 The Master and His Dogs

Day 1
Read the fable below. Then fill in the blanks on the next page.

A country man ____1____ snowed into his country house by a ____2____ storm. First he
killed his sheep, ____3____ then his goats, to keep his household ____4____. As the storm
continued, he was obliged ____5____ slaughter his yoke oxen for food.

On ____6____ this, his dogs met together and said: "____7____ is time for us to be off, ____8____
if the master does not spare his ____9____, who work for his gain, how can ____10____ expect
him to spare us?"

He is ____11____ to be trusted as a friend who mistreats ____12____ own family.

_____

Day 2
Interesting and curious words

1.   Read the fable, and write the meaning of each word below.

  a. spare _____

  b. mistreat _____

  c. yoke _____

  2.   Check your answers in the answer key on p.192. Use a dictionary to find other meanings
for the words.

  3.   Below, write a sentence using each word as it is used in the fable.

  a. _____

  _____

  b. _____

  _____

  c. _____

  _____

Lesson 29 The Master and His Dogs

Day 1
Fill in the blanks. Write your answers below.

1. _____

2. _____

3. _____

4. _____

5. _____

6. _____

7. _____

8. _____

9. _____

10. _____

11. _____

12. _____

Correct exact words   _____
Correct appropriate words   _____
Total correct words   _____

Day 2
Questions for understanding: Write your answers below.

1. What will this man's life be like when spring comes?

_____

_____

_____

_____

2. How could this man have avoided his difficulty?

_____

_____

_____

_____

Lesson 30 The Donkey and the Old Shepherd

Day 1
Read the fable below. Then fill in the blanks on the next page.

A shepherd was watching ____1____ donkey feeding in a meadow, Suddenly the _____2___ was alarmed by the cries of his ____3____ enemy. He appealed to the donkey: "Come ____4____ us run. Hide with me so that we ____5____ not be captured by my enemy."

The ____6____ lazily replied, "Why should I, pray? Do ____7____ think it likely the conqueror will place ____8____ the load on me?"

"No," rejoined the ____9____ .

"Then," said the donkey, "as long as ____10____ carry the same load, what does it ____11____ to me whom I serve?"

In a ____12____ of government, the very poor change nothing ____13____ the name of their master.

Day 2
Interesting and curious words

1. Read the fable, and write the meaning of each word below.
a. appealed _____

b. alarmed _____

c. rejoined_____

2. Check your answers in the answer key on p.192. Use a dictionary to find other meanings for the words.

3.Below, write a sentence using each word as it is used in the fable.

a. _____

_____

b. _____

_____

c. _____

_____

Lesson 30 The Donkey and the Old Shepherd

Day 1
Fill in the blanks. Write your answers below.

1. _____

2. _____

3. _____

4. _____

5. _____

6. _____

7. _____

8. _____

9. _____

10. _____

11. _____

12. _____

13. _____

Correct exact words   _____

Correct appropriate words   _____

Total correct words   _____

Day 2
Questions for understanding: Write your answers below.

1. Why didn't the donkey want to run and hide?

_____

_____

_____

_____

2. What lesson can you learn from this fable?

_____

_____

_____

_____

Lesson 31 The Thief and the Housedog

Day 1
Read the fable below. Then fill in the blanks on the next page.

A thief came ____1____ the night to break into a house. ____2____ brought with him several slices of meat ____3____ order to pacify the dog, so that ____4____ would not alarm his master by barking.

____5____ the thief threw him the pieces of ____6____, the dog said, "If you think a ____7____ meat will stop me from barking to ____8____ my master, you will be greatly mistaken. ____9____ sudden kindness at your hands will only ____10____ me more watchful. I suspect that with ____11____ unexpected favors to me, you wish to ____12____ friends so you can do my master ____13____ great harm."

Beware of gifts from strangers.

Day 2
Interesting and curious words

1. Read the fable, and write the meaning of each word below.

  a. pacify _____

  b. alert _____

  c. beware _____

2. Check your answers in the answer key on p.192. Use a dictionary to find other meanings for the words.

3. Below, write a sentence using each word as it is used in the fable.

  a. _____

  _____

  b. _____

  _____

  c. _____

  _____

Lesson 31 The Thief and the Housedog

Day 1
Fill in the blanks. Write your answers below.

1. _____

2. _____

3. _____

4. _____

5. _____

6. _____

7. _____

8. _____

9. _____

10. _____

11. _____

12. _____

13. _____

Correct exact words   _____

Correct appropriate words   _____

Total correct words   _____

Day 2
Questions for understanding: Write your answers below.

1. Why was the dog alerted by the stranger?

_____

_____

_____

_____

2. What is this fable telling you about gifts from strangers?

_____

_____

_____

_____

Lesson 32 The Horse and the Donkey

Day 1
Read the fable below. Then fill in the blanks on the next page.

A horse, proud ____1____ his fine ribbons and silver saddle, met ____2____ donkey on the highway. The donkey, being ____3____ laden, moved slowly out of the way.

"____4____ can hardly resist kicking you with my ____5____," said the horse.

The donkey held ____6____ peace and made only a silent appeal ____7____ the justice of the gods. Not long ____8____, the horse, having become broken-winded, was ____9____ by his owner to the farm.

The ____10____, seeing him drawing a dung cart, thus derided ____11____: "Where, O boastful horse, are now all ____12____ fancy trappings? You are reduced to the ____13____ you so lately treated with contempt."

_____

Day 2
Interesting and curious words

1. Read the fable, and write the meaning of each word below.

a. peace _____

b. derided _____

c. trappings _____

2. Check your answers in the answer key on p.192. Use a dictionary to find other meanings for the words.

3. Below, write a sentence using each word as it is used in the fable.

a. _____

_____

b. _____

_____

c. _____

_____

Lesson 32 The Horse and the Donkey

Day 1
Fill in the blanks. Write your answers below.

1. _____

2. _____

3. _____

4. _____

5. _____

6. _____

7. _____

8. _____

9. _____

10. _____

11. _____

12. _____

13. _____

Correct exact words   _____

Correct appropriate words   _____

Total correct words   _____

Day 2
Questions for understanding: Write your answers below.

1. If you were the donkey in this fable, what would you do?

_____

_____

_____

_____

2. What is this fable trying to tell you about arrogance?

_____

_____

_____

_____

Lesson 33 The Old Man and Death

Day 1
Read the fable below. Then fill in the blanks on the next page.

An old ____1____ was employed in cutting wood in the ____2____ and carrying the firewood to the city ____3____ sale. One day, he became much wearied with ____4____ long journey. He sat down by the wayside ____5____, throwing down his load, said, "Oh, I ____6____ so tired. I wish Death would ____7____."

Death immediately appeared in answer to ____8____ summons and asked, "You called me? What is ____9____ that you want, old man?"

The old ____10____ hurriedly replied, "That you help me to ____11____ up this load and place it again ____12____ my shoulders."

Watch what you pray for: you ____13____ get it.

Interesting and curious words

1.   Read the fable, and write the meaning of each word below.

   a. wearied _____

   b. summon _____

   c. wayside _____

2.   Check your answers in the answer key on p.192. Use a dictionary to find other meanings for the words.

3.   Below, write a sentence using each word as it is used in the fable.

   a. _____

   _____

   b. _____

   _____

   c. _____

   _____

Lesson 33 The Old Man and Death

Fill in the blanks. Write your answers below.

1. _____   8. _____

2. _____   9. _____

3. _____   10. _____

4. _____   11. _____

5. _____   12. _____

6. _____   13. _____

7. _____

Correct exact words   _____

Correct appropriate words   _____

Total correct words   _____

Day 2
Questions for understanding: Write your answers below.

1. How did the old man feel at the beginning of the fable?

_____

_____

_____

_____

2. Why did the old man want to pick up his load of wood again?

_____

_____

_____

_____

Lesson 34 The Widow and the Sheep

Day 1
Read the fable below. Then fill in the blanks on the next page.

A poor widow ____1____ one solitary sheep. At shearing time, wishing ____2____ take his fleece and to avoid expense, ____3____ sheared him herself, but used the shears ____4____ unskillfully that with the fleece she sheared ____5____ flesh.

The sheep, writhing with pain, said, "____6____ do you hurt me so, Mistress? What ____7____ can my blood add to the wool? ____8____ you want my flesh, there is the ____9____, who will kill me in an instant. ____10____ if you want my fleece and wool, ____11____ is the shearer, who will shear and ____12____ hurt me."

The cheapest method does not ____13____ give the greatest gain.

_____

Day 2
Interesting and curious words

1.   Read the fable, and write the meaning of each word below.

   a. solitary _____

   b. fleece _____

   c. shearing _____

2.   Check your answers in the answer key on p.192. Use a dictionary to find other meanings
        for the words.

3.   Below, write a sentence using each word as it is used in the fable.

   a. _____

   _____

   b. _____

   _____

   c. _____

   _____

Lesson 34 The Widow and the Sheep

Day 1
Fill in the blanks. Write your answers below.

1. _____

2. _____

3. _____

4. _____

5. _____

6. _____

7. _____

8. _____

9. _____

10. _____

11. _____

12. _____

13. _____

Correct exact words _____

Correct appropriate words _____

Total correct words _____

Day 2
Questions for understanding: Write your answers below.

1. What was the widow in this fable trying to do?

_____

_____

_____

_____

2. What is this fable trying to show you?

_____

_____

_____

_____

Lesson 35 The Crow and the Pitcher

Day 1
Read the fable below. Then fill in the blanks on the next page.

A ____1____ who was dying of thirst saw a pitcher ____2____, hoping to find water, flew to it ____3____ delight. When he reached it, he discovered ____4____ his grief that it contained so little ____5____ that he could not possibly get at ____6____.

He tried everything he could think of ____7____ reach the water, but all his efforts were ____8____ vain. At last he collected as many ____9____ as he could carry with his beak ____10____ dropped the stones one by one into the ____11____, until he brought the water within his ____12____ and thus saved his life.

Necessity is ____13____ mother of invention.

_____

Day 2
Interesting and curious words

1. Read the fable, and write the meaning of each word below.
    a. delight _____

    b. grief _____

    c. invention _____

2. Check your answers in the answer key on p.192. Use a dictionary to find other meanings for the words.

3. Below, write a sentence using each word as it is used in the fable.

a. _____

_____

b. _____

_____

c. _____

_____

Lesson 35 The Crow and the Pitcher

Day 1
Fill in the blanks. Write your answers below.

1. _____

2. _____

3. _____

4. _____

5. _____

6. _____

7. _____

8. _____

9. _____

10. _____

11. _____

12. _____

13. _____

Correct exact words   _____

Correct appropriate words   _____

Total correct words   _____

Day 2
Questions for understanding: Write your answers below.

1. How would you describe the crow in this fable?

_____

_____

_____

_____

2. What does this fable tell you about solving problems?

_____

_____

_____

_____

Lesson 36 The Hawk and the Nightingale

Day 1
Read the fable below. Then fill in the blanks on the next page.

A nightingale was sitting ____1____ up on an oak and singing his ____2____ song. He was seen by a ____3____ who, being in need of food, swooped ____4____ and caught the nightingale.

The nightingale, about to ____5____ his life, begged the hawk to let him ____6____, saying, "I am not big enough to ____7____ the hunger of a hawk. If you want ____8____, you should pursue the larger birds."

The ____9____, interrupting him, said: "I should indeed have ____10____ my senses if I should let go ____11____ already in my hand, for the sake ____12____ pursuing birds that are not yet even __ ____13____ sight."

_____

Day 2
Interesting and curious words

1.   Read the fable, and write the meaning of each word below.

a. swooped _____

b. satisfy _____

c. pursuing _____

2.   Check your answers in the answer key on p.192 Use a dictionary to find other meanings for the words.

3.   Below, write a sentence using each word as it is used in the fable.

a. _____

_____

b. _____

_____

c. _____

_____

Lesson 36 The Hawk and the Nightingale

Day 1
Fill in the blanks. Write your answers below.

1. _____

2. _____

3. _____

4. _____

5. _____

6. _____

7. _____

8. _____

9. _____

10. _____

11. _____

12. _____

13. _____

Correct exact words   _____

Correct appropriate words _____

Total correct words   _____

Day 2
Questions for understanding: Write your answers below.

1. What was the error in the nightingale's reasoning?

_____

_____

_____

_____

2. What lesson can you learn from this fable?

_____

_____

_____

_____

Lesson 37 The Monkey and the Camel

Day 1
Read the fable below. Then fill in the blanks on the next page.

The beasts of ____1____ forest gave a splendid party at which ____2____ monkey stood up and danced. The monkey's ____3____ vastly delighted the assembly. He sat down ____4____ universal applause.

The camel became envious of ____5____ praise bestowed on the monkey. He wanted ____6____ divert the attention of the guests to ____7____, He proposed to stand up in his ____8____ and dance for their amusement. The camel ____9____ about in such an utterly silly manner ____10____ the beasts, in a fit of indignation, ____11____ upon him with clubs and drove him ____12____ of the assembly.

Develop your own skills; ____13____ is foolish to imitate your betters.

Day 2
Interesting and curious words

1. Read the fable, and write the meaning of each word below.

   a. divert _____

   b. utterly _____

   c. indignation_____

2. Check your answers in the answer key on p.193. Use a dictionary to find other meanings for the words.

3. Below, write a sentence using each word as it is used in the fable.

   a. _____

   _____

   b. _____

   _____

   c. _____

   _____

82

Lesson 37 The Monkey and the Camel

Day 1
Fill in the blanks. Write your answers below.

1. _____   8. _____

2. _____   9. _____

3. _____   10. _____

4. _____   11. _____

5. _____   12. _____

6. _____   13. _____

7. _____

Correct exact words   _____

Correct appropriate words   _____

Total correct words   _____

Day 2
Questions for understanding: Write your answers below.

1. Why did the camel act as he did?

_____

_____

_____

_____

2. What could the camel have done differently to get respect?

_____

_____

_____

_____

Lesson 38 The Spendthrift and the Swallow

Day 1
Read the fable below. Then fill in the blanks on the next page.

A ____1____ man, a great spendthrift, had run through ____2____ his inheritance and had only one good coat ____3____. One day he happened to see a ____4____, which had appeared early, before its season. ____5____ swallow was skimming along a pool and twittering ____6____.

The young man supposed that spring had ____7____. He went and sold his cloak. Not ____8____ days later, winter set in again with ____9____ frost and cold. When he found the ____10____ swallow lifeless on the ground, the young man said: "____11____ bird! What have you done? By appearing ____12____ the springtime, you have not only killed ____13____, but you have wrought my destruction also."

_____

Day 2
Interesting and curious words

1. Read the fable, and write the meaning of each word below.

a. spendthrift _____

b. wrought _____

c. twittering _____

2.   Check your answers in the answer key on p.193. Use a dictionary to find other meanings for the words.

3.   Below, write a sentence using each word as it is used in the fable.

a. _____

   _____

b. _____

   _____

c. _____

   _____

Lesson 38 The Spendthrift and the Swallow

Day 1
Fill in the blanks. Write your answers below.

1. _____

2. _____

3. _____

4. _____

5. _____

6. _____

7. _____

8. _____

9. _____

10. _____

11. _____

12. _____

13. _____

Correct exact words   _____

Correct appropriate words   _____

Total correct words   _____

Day 2
Questions for understanding: Write your answers below.

1. Do you think the swallow is responsible for the man's misery?

_____

_____

_____

_____

2. What is this fable trying to tell you about snap judgments?

_____

_____

_____

_____

Lesson 39 The Kid and the Wolf

Day 1
Read the fable below. Then fill in the blanks on the next page.

A kid, returning ____1____ protection from the pasture, was pursued by ____2____ wolf. Seeing he could not escape, he ____3____ around, and said: "I know, friend Wolf, ____4____ I must be your prey, but before ____5____ die, I would ask of you one ____6____. Will you play me a tune so ____7____ may dance?"

The wolf complied and, ____8____ he was piping and the kid was ____9____, some hounds, hearing the sound, ran up ____10____ began chasing the wolf. Turning to the kid, he ____11____, "It is just what I deserve, for ____12____, who am only a butcher, should not ____13____ turned piper just to please you."

_____

Day 2
Interesting and curious words

1.   Read the fable, and write the meaning of each word below.

a. prey _____

b. favor _____

c. complied _____

2.   Check your answers in the answer key on p.193. Use a dictionary to find other meanings for the words.

3.   Below, write a sentence using each word as it is used in the fable.

a. _____

_____

b. _____

_____

c. _____

_____

Lesson 39 The Kid and the Wolf

Day 1
Fill in the blanks. Write your answers below.

1. _____   8. _____

2. _____   9. _____

3. _____   10. _____

4. _____   11. _____

5. _____   12. _____

6. _____   13. _____

7. _____

Correct exact words   _____

Correct appropriate words _____

Total correct words   _____

Day 2
Questions for understanding: Write your answers below.

1. What was the wolf's mistake in this fable?

_____

_____

_____

_____

2. What is the main idea of this fable?

_____

_____

_____

_____

Lesson 40 The Boasting Traveler

Day 1
Read the fable below. Then fill in the blanks on the next page.

A man who ____1____ traveled in foreign lands boasted a lot ____2____ he returned to his own country, He ____3____ of the many wonderful and heroic feats ____4____ had performed in the different places he ___5___ visited.

Among other things, he said, "When I ___6___ in Rhodes, I leapt such a distance ___7___ that no man in Rhodes could leap anywhere ___8___ as far. Many people in Rhodes saw ___9___ do it, and I can call them ___10___ witnesses."

One of the bystanders interrupted him, ____11____, "Now, my good man, if this be ___12___, there is no need of witnesses. Suppose ____13____ to be Rhodes, and leap for us."

Day 2

Interesting and curious words

1.   Read the fable, and write the meaning of each word below.

  a. heroic _____

  b. leapt _____

  c. witnesses _____

2.   Check your answers in the answer key on p.193. Use a dictionary to find other meanings for the words.

3.   Below, write a sentence using each word as it is used in the fable.

  a. _____

  _____

  b. _____

  _____

  c. _____

  _____

Lesson 40 The Boasting Traveler

Day 1
Fill in the blanks. Write your answers below.

1. _____

2. _____

3. _____

4. _____

5. _____

6. _____

7. _____

8. _____

9. _____

10. _____

11. _____

12. _____

13. _____

Correct exact words   _____

Correct appropriate words   _____

Total correct words   _____

Day 2
Questions for understanding: Write your answers below.

1. Why did the traveler tell about his feats that happened in foreign lands?

_____

_____

_____

_____

2. What does this fable tell you about treating boastful people?

_____

_____

_____

_____

Lesson 41 The Trees and the Axe

Day 1
Read the fable below. Then fill in the blanks on the next page.

A man _____1_____ into a forest and asked the trees _____2_____ provide him a handle for his axe. _____3_____ trees consented to his request and gave _____4_____ a young ash tree.

No sooner had _____5_____ man fitted a new handle to his _____6_____ from the ash tree, than he began _____7_____ use it and quickly felled with his _____8_____ the noblest giants of the forest.

An _____9_____ oak, lamenting too late the destruction _____10_____ his companions, said to a neighboring cedar, "_____11_____ first step has lost us all. If _____12_____ had not given up the rights of the _____13_____, we might yet have retained our own _____14_____ and have stood for ages."

_____

Day 2
Interesting and curious words

1.   Read the fable, and write the meaning of each word below.

   a. felled _____

   b. lamenting _____

   c. retained _____

2.   Check your answers in the answer key on p.193. Use a dictionary to find other meanings for the words.

3.   Below, write a sentence using each word as it is used in the fable.

   a. _____

   _____

   b. _____

   _____

   c. _____

   _____

Lesson 41 The Trees and the Axe

Day 1
Fill in the blanks. Write your answers below.

1. _____   8. _____

2. _____   9. _____

3. _____   10. _____

4. _____   11. _____

5. _____   12. _____

6. _____   13. _____

7. _____   14. _____

Correct exact words   _____
Correct appropriate words   _____
Total correct words   _____

Day 2
Questions for understanding: Write your answers below.

1. What does this fable tell you about granting small favors?

_____

_____

_____

_____

2. What does this fable tell you about individual rights?

_____

_____

_____

_____

Lesson 42 The Two Travelers and the Axe

Day 1
Read the fable below. Then fill in the blanks on the next page.

Two men, Henry and William, ____1____ journeying together. Henry picked up ____2____ axe that lay upon the path, and ____3____, "I have found an axe."

"No, my ____4____," replied William. "Do not say, 'I,' ____5____ say, 'We have found an axe.'"
They had ____6____ gone far before they saw the owner ____7____ the axe pursuing them, and Henry, who ____8____ had picked up the axe, said, "We ____9____ been caught."

"No," replied William, "keep ____10____ your first mode of speech, my friend.
____11____ said 'I have found an axe.' Now ____12____ should say, 'I have been caught.' Do ____13____ say, 'We have been caught.'"

He ____14____ shares the prize should share the danger.

Day 2

Interesting and curious words

1.   Read the fable, and write the meaning of each word below.

   a. journeying _____

   b. mode _____

2.   Check your answers in the answer key on p.193. Use a dictionary to find other meanings for the words.

3.   Below, write a sentence using each word as it is used in the fable.

   a. _____

   _____

   b. _____

   _____

Lesson 42 The Two Travelers and the Axe

Day 1
Fill in the blanks. Write your answers below.

1. _____

2. _____

3. _____

4. _____

5. _____

6. _____

7. _____

8. _____

9. _____

10. _____

11. _____

12. _____

13. _____

14. _____

Correct exact words _____

Correct appropriate words _____

Total correct words _____

Day 2
Questions for understanding: Write your answers below.

1. What should Henry and William have done when they found the axe?

_____

_____

_____

_____

2. What kind of person is William?

_____

_____

_____

_____

Lesson 43 The Man and His Two Sweethearts

Day 1
Read the fable below. Then fill in the blanks on the next page.

A middle-aged man, whose ____1____ had begun to turn gray, courted two
____2____ at the same time. One of them ____3____ young, and the other well advanced in
____4____. The elder woman, ashamed to be courted ____5____ a man younger than herself,
made a point, ____6____ her admirer visited her, to pull out ____7____ portion of his black hairs.

The younger, ____8____ the contrary, not wishing to become the ____9____ of an old man, was
equally zealous ____10____ removing every gray hair she could find. ____11____ it came to
pass that between them ____12____ he very soon found that he had ____13____ a hair left on his
head.

Those ____14____ seek to please everybody please nobody.

Day 2

Interesting and curious words

1.   Read the fable, and write the meaning of each word below.

   a. courted _____

   b. advanced _____

   c. zealous _____

2.   Check your answers in the answer key on p.193. Use a dictionary to find other meanings
        for the words.

3.   Below, write a sentence using each word as it is used in the fable.

   a. _____

   _____

   b. _____

   _____

   c. _____

   _____

Lesson 43 The Man and His Two Sweethearts

Day 1
Fill in the blanks. Write your answers below.

1. _____   8. _____

2. _____   9. _____

3. _____   10. _____

4. _____   11. _____

5. _____   12. _____

6. _____   13. _____

7. _____   14. _____

Correct exact words   _____
Correct appropriate words   _____
Total correct words   _____

Day 2
Questions for understanding: Write your answers below.

1. What kind of man does this fable portray?

_____

_____

_____

_____

2. What does this fable tell you about the character of the two women?

_____

_____

_____

_____

Lesson 44 The Weasel and the Mice

Day 1
Read the fable below. Then fill in the blanks on the next page.

A weasel was ____1____ old and weak and was not able ____2____ catch mice as well as he once ____3____. He rolled himself in flour and laid ____4____ in a dark corner of the barn.

____5____ mouse, supposing him to be food, leaped ____6____ him and was instantly caught and squeezed ____7____ death. Another mouse perished in a similar ____8____, and then a third, and still others ____9____ them.

A very old mouse, who had ____10____ many a trap and snare, observed from ____11____ safe distance the trick of the crafty ____12____ and said, "Ah! You that lie there, may you ____13____ just in the same proportion as you ____14____ are what you pretend to be!"

_____

Day 2

Interesting and curious words

1.   Read the fable, and write the meaning of each word below.

   a. supposing _____

   b. snare _____

   c. crafty _____

2.   Check your answers in the answer key on p.193. Use a dictionary to find other meanings for the words.

3.   Below, write a sentence using each word as it is used in the fable.

   a. _____

   _____

   b. _____

   _____

   c. _____

   _____

Lesson 44 The Weasel and the Mice

Day 1
Fill in the blanks. Write your answers below.

1. _____

2. _____

3. _____

4. _____

5. _____

6. _____

7. _____

8. _____

9. _____

10. _____

11. _____

12. _____

13. _____

14. _____

Correct exact words   _____

Correct appropriate words   _____

Total correct words   _____

Day 2
Questions for understanding: Write your answers below.

1. What do you think of the mice that fell for the weasel's trick?

_____

_____

_____

_____

2. What does the old mouse mean by his comment to the weasel?

_____

_____

_____

_____

Lesson 45 The Mischievous Dog

Day 1
Read the fable below. Then fill in the blanks on the next page.

A ____1____ herding dog used to run up quietly ____2____ the heels of everyone he met and ____3____ them without notice. His master tied a bell ____4____ his neck so the dog might warn ____5____ of his presence wherever he went. The ____6____ thought it was a mark of distinction ____7____ grew proud of his bell. He went ____8____ tinkling it all over the marketplace.

One ____9____ an old hound said to him, "Why ____10____ you make such an exhibition of yourself? ____11____ bell that you carry is not any ____12____ of merit, but on the contrary a mark ____13____ disgrace, It is a public notice to ____14____ men to avoid you as an ill-mannered ____15____."

Notoriety is often mistaken for fame.

_____

Day 2
Interesting and curious words

1. Read the fable, and write the meaning of each word below.

    a. merit _____

    b. distinction _____

    c. notoriety _____

2. Check your answers in the answer key on p.193. Use a dictionary to find other meanings for the words.

3. Below, write a sentence using each word as it is used in the fable.

a. _____

_____

b. _____

_____

c. _____

_____

Lesson 45 The Mischievous Dog

Day 1
Fill in the blanks Write your answers below

1. _____
2. _____
3. _____
4. _____
5. _____
6. _____
7. _____
8. _____

9. _____
10. _____
11. _____
12. _____
13. _____
14. _____
15. _____

Correct exact words   _____
Correct appropriate words   _____
Total correct words   _____

Day 2
Questions for understanding: Write your answers below.

1. What does this fable say about people who wear fancy clothes?

_____

_____

_____

_____

2. Can you think of people to whom this fable applies?

_____

_____

_____

_____

Lesson 46 The Rabbits and the Frogs

Day 1
Read the fable below. Then fill in the blanks on the next page.

The rabbits were oppressed ____1____ their own exceeding timidity and weary of ____2____ perpetual alarm to which they were exposed. ____3____ all agreed to put an end to ____4____ troubles by jumping from a lofty precipice ____5____ a deep lake below.

They scampered ____6____ in large numbers to carry out their ____7____. The frogs lying on the banks of ____8____ lake heard the noise of their feet ____9____ rushed helter-skelter to the deep water for ____10____.

On seeing the rapid disappearance of the ____11____, one of the rabbits cried out to ____12____ companions: "Wait, my friends, do not do ____13____ you intended, for you now see that ____14____ are creatures who are still more timid ____15____ ourselves."

Day 2
Interesting and curious words

1.   Read the fable, and write the meaning of each word below.

   a. timidity _____

   b. perpetual _____

   c. scampered _____

2.   Check your answers in the answer key on p.193. Use a dictionary to find other meanings for the words.

3.   Below, write a sentence using each word as it is used in the fable.

   a. _____

   _____

   b. _____

   _____

   c. _____

   _____

100

Lesson 46 The Rabbits and the Frogs

Day 1
Fill in the blanks Write your answers below

1. _____

2. _____

3. _____

4. _____

5. _____

6. _____

7. _____

8. _____

9. _____

10. _____

11. _____

12. _____

13. _____

14. _____

15. _____

Correct exact words

Correct appropriate words   _____

Total correct words   _____

                              _____

Day 2
Questions for understanding: Write your answers below.

1. What does this fable tell you about fear and anxiety?

_____

_____

_____

_____

2. Why did the rabbits change their minds?

_____

_____

_____

_____

Lesson 47 The Ant and the Dove

Day 1
Read the fable below. Then fill in the blanks on the next page.

An ant ____1____ to the bank of a river to quench ____2____ thirst. She fell in and was ____3____ carried away by the rush of the ____4____. The ant was on the point of ____5____, when a dove sitting on a tree ____6____ over the water, plucked a leaf and ____7____ it fall into the stream close to ____8____. The ant climbed onto the leaf and floated ____9____ to the bank.

Shortly afterward, a bird catcher ____10____ and stood under the tree. He laid ____11____ trap for the dove, which sat in ____12____ branches. The ant, perceiving his design, stung ____13____ bird catcher on the foot. In pain, the ____14____ threw down his trap, and the ____15____ made the dove fly away.

_____

Day 2

Interesting and curious words

1. Read the fable, and write the meaning of each word below.

   a. quench _____

   b. plucked _____

   c. design _____

2. Check your answers in the answer key on p.193. Use a dictionary to find other meanings for the words.

3. Below, write a sentence using each word as it is used in the fable.

   a. _____

   _____

   b. _____

   _____

   c. _____

   _____

Lesson 47 The Ant and the Dove

Fill in the blanks Write your answers below

1. _____   9. _____

2. _____   10. _____

3. _____   11. _____

4. _____   12. _____

5. _____   13. _____

6. _____   14. _____

7. _____   15. _____

8. _____

Correct exact words   _____
Correct appropriate words   _____
Total correct words   _____

Day 2
Questions for understanding: Write your answers below.

1. What does this fable tell you about the character of the dove?

_____

_____

_____

_____

2. What can you learn about doing good deeds from this fable?

_____

_____

_____

_____

Lesson 48 The Crow and the Raven

Day 1
Read the fable below. Then fill in the blanks on the next page.

A crow _____1_____ jealous of a raven, because he was _____2_____ a bird of good omen. The raven _____3_____ attracted the attention of men, who thought, _____4_____ his flight or his call, he predicted _____5_____ good or evil course of future events.

_____6_____ some travelers approaching, the crow flew up _____7_____ a tree, and perching herself on one _____8_____ the branches, cawed as loudly as she _____9_____ .

One traveler turned towards the sound and _____10_____ , "What is that? What does it forebode?"

_____11_____ other traveler said to his companion, "Let _____12_____ proceed on our journey, my friend, for _____13_____ is only the caw of a foolish _____14_____ , and her cry, you know, is no _____15_____ ."

Those who attempt to assume a character that does not belong to them only make themselves ridiculous.

_____

Day 2
Interesting and curious words

1.   Read the fable, and write the meaning of each word below.

  a. omen _____

  b. forebode _____

2.   Check your answers in the answer key on p.193. Use a dictionary to find other meanings for the words.

3.   Below, write a sentence using each word as it is used in the fable.

  a. _____

  _____

  b. _____

  _____

Lesson 48 The Crow and the Raven

Day 1

Fill in the blanks Write your answers below

1. _____

2. _____

3. _____

4. _____

5. _____

6. _____

7. _____

8. _____

9. _____

10. _____

11. _____

12. _____

13. _____

14. _____

15. _____

Correct exact words   _____

Correct appropriate words   _____

Total correct words   _____

Day 2

Questions for understanding: Write your answers below.

1. What do you think about omens?

_____

_____

_____

_____

2. What does this fable tell you about people who imitate others?

_____

_____

_____

_____

Lesson 49 The North Wind and the Sun

Day 1
Read the fable below. Then fill in the blanks on the next page.

The North Wind ___1___ the Sun argued as to which was ___2___ most powerful. They finally agreed that he ___3___ could first strip a wayfaring man of ___4___ clothes should be declared the victor.

The ___5___ Wind first tried his power and blew ___6___ all his might, but the keener his ___7___, the closer the traveler wrapped his cloak ___8___ him, until at last, resigning all hope ___9___ victory, the North Wind called upon the Sun ___10___ see what he could do.

The Sun ___11___ shone out with all his warmth. The ___12___ no sooner felt his genial rays than ___13___ took off one garment after another, and ___14___ last, fairly overcome with heat, undressed and ___15___ in a stream that lay in his path.

Persuasion is better than force.

_____

Day 2

Interesting and curious words

1.   Read the fable, and write the meaning of each word below.

   a. wayfaring _____

   b. genial _____

   c. keener _____

2.   Check your answers in the answer key on p.194. Use a dictionary to find other meanings for the words.

3.   Below, write a sentence using each word as it is used in the fable.

   a. _____

   _____

   b. _____

   _____

   c. _____

   _____

Lesson 49 The North Wind and the Sun

Day 1

Fill in the blanks Write your answers below

1. _____
2. _____
3. _____
4. _____
5. _____
6. _____
7. _____
8. _____

9. _____
10. _____
11. _____
12. _____
13. _____
14. _____
15. _____

Correct exact words   _____
Correct appropriate words   _____
Total correct words   _____

Day 2

Questions for understanding: Write your answers below.

1. Can you think of a way the North Wind might have won the argument?

_____

_____

_____

_____

2. Write about an example of this fable from real life.

_____

_____

_____

_____

Lesson 50 The Fox and the Crow

Day 1
Read the fable below. Then fill in the blanks on the next page.

A crow ____1____ stolen a bit of meat, perched in ____2____ tree and held it in her beak. ____3____ fox, seeing this, longed to possess the ____4____ himself, and by a wily stratagem succeeded.

" ____5____ handsome is the crow," he exclaimed, "in ____6____ beauty of her shape and in the ____7____ of her complexion! Oh, if her voice ____8____ only equal to her beauty, she would ____9____ considered the queen of birds!"

This he ____10____ deceitfully, but the crow, anxious to refute ____11____ reflection cast upon her voice, set up ____12____ loud caw and dropped the flesh.

The ____13____ quickly picked it up and thus addressed ____14____ crow: "My good crow, your voice is good ____15____, but your wit is wanting."

The flatterer seeks only his own good.

_____

Day 2
Interesting and curious words

1.   Read the fable, and write the meaning of each word below.

a. stratagem _____

b. refute _____

c. wit _____

2.   Check your answers in the answer key on p.194. Use a dictionary to find other meanings for the words.

3.   Below, write a sentence using each word as it is used in the fable.

a. _____

_____

b. _____

_____

c. _____

_____

108

Lesson 50 The Fox and the Crow

Day 1
Fill in the blanks Write your answers below

1. _____   9. _____

2. _____   10. _____

3. _____   11. _____

4. _____   12. _____

5. _____   13. _____

6. _____   14. _____

7. _____   15. _____

8. _____

Correct exact words   _____
Correct appropriate words   _____
Total correct words   _____

Day 2
Questions for understanding: Write your answers below.

1. What is the character of the crow in this fable?

_____

_____

_____

_____

2. What does this fable teach you about flattery?

_____

_____

_____

_____

Lesson 51 The Donkey and His Purchaser

Day 1
Read the fable below. Then fill in the blanks on the next page.

A man ____1____ to purchase a donkey and agreed with ____2____ owner that he should try out the ____3____ before he bought him. He took the ____4____ home and put him in the barnyard ____5____ his other donkeys. The new animal ignored ____6____ the others and immediately went to join ____7____ one that was most idle and the ____8____ eater of them all.

Seeing this, the ____9____ put a halter on the donkey and led ____10____ back to his owner. The owner asked ____11____ he could have made a trial of ____12____, in so short a time. The man answered, "____13____ do not need a trial; I know ____14____ he will be just the same as ____15____ one he chose for his companion."

_____

Day 2
Interesting and curious words

1.   Read the fable, and write the meaning of each word below.

  a. idle _____

  b. halter _____

2.   Check your answers in the answer key on p.194. Use a dictionary to find other meanings for the words.

3.   Below, write a sentence using each word as it is used in the fable.

  a. _____

  _____

  b. _____

  _____

110

Lesson 51 The Donkey and His Purchaser

Day 1
Fill in the blanks Write your answers below

1. _____

2. _____

3. _____

4. _____

5. _____

6. _____

7. _____

8. _____

9. _____

10. _____

11. _____

12. _____

13. _____

14. _____

15. _____

Correct exact words   _____

Correct appropriate words   _____

Total correct words   _____

Day 2
Questions for understanding: Write your answers below.

1. Why did the donkey seek out his companion?

_____

_____

_____

_____

2. What does this fable tell you about choosing your associates?

_____

_____

_____

_____

Lesson 52 The Peasant and the Apple Tree

Day 1
Read the fable below. Then fill in the blanks on the next page.

A peasant ____1____ an apple tree in his garden that ____2____ no fruit, but served only as a harbor ____3____ the sparrows and grasshoppers. He resolved to ____4____ it down. Taking his axe in his ____5____ , made a bold stroke at its roots.

____6____ grasshoppers and sparrows entreated him not to cut ____7____ the tree that sheltered them. If the peasant would ____8____ it, they would sing to him and ____9____ his labors. He paid no attention to ____10____ , but gave the tree a second and ____11____ third blow with his axe.

When he ____12____ the hollow of the tree, he found ____13____ hive full of honey. Having tasted the ____14____ , he put down his axe, and looking ____15____ the tree as sacred, took great care ____16____ it.

Self-interest alone moves some men.

Day 2
Interesting and curious words

1.   Read the fable, and write the meaning of each word below.

a. harbor _____

b. entreated _____

c. resolved _____

2.   Check your answers in the answer key on p.194. Use a dictionary to find other meanings for the words.

3.   Below, write a sentence using each word as it is used in the fable.

a. _____

_____

b. _____

_____

c. _____

_____

Lesson 52 The Peasant and the Apple Tree

Day 1

Fill in the blanks Write your answers below

1. _____
2. _____
3. _____
4. _____
5. _____
6. _____
7. _____
8. _____

9. _____
10. _____
11. _____
12. _____
13. _____
14. _____
15. _____
16. _____

Correct exact words   _____

Correct appropriate words   _____

Total correct words   _____

Day 2

Questions for understanding: Write your answers below.

1. How do you think this peasant treats other people?

_____

_____

_____

_____

2. What is the man in this fable like?

_____

_____

_____

_____

Lesson 53 The Mules and the Robbers

Day 1
Read the fable below. Then fill in the blanks on the next page.

Two mules well-laden ____1____ packs were trudging along. One carried panniers ____2____ with money, the other sacks of grain. The ____3____ carrying the treasure walked with head erect, ____4____ if conscious of the value of his ____5____, and tossed up and down the clear-toned ____6____ fastened to his neck. His companion followed ____7____ quiet and easy step.

All of a ____8____, robbers rushed upon them from their hiding-____9____, and in the scuffle with their owners, ____10____ mule carrying the treasure was wounded with a ____11____. The robbers greedily seized the treasure while taking ____12____ notice of the grain. The mule that ____13____ been robbed and wounded bewailed his misfortunes. ____14____ other mule replied, "I am indeed glad ____15____ I was thought so little of, for I have ____16____ nothing, nor was I wounded."

_____

Day 2

Interesting and curious words

1.   Read the fable, and write the meaning of each word below.

   a. panniers _____

   b. scuffle _____

   c. bewailed _____

2.   Check your answers in the answer key on p.194. Use a dictionary to find other meanings for the words.

3.   Below, write a sentence using each word as it is used in the fable.

   a. _____

   _____

   b. _____

   _____

   c. _____

   _____

114

Lesson 53 The Mules and the Robbers

Day 1
Fill in the blanks Write your answers below

1. _____   9. _____

2. _____   10. _____

3. _____   11. _____

4. _____   12. _____

5. _____   13. _____

6. _____   14. _____

7. _____   15. _____

8. _____   16. _____

Correct exact words   _____
Correct appropriate words   _____
Total correct words   _____

Day 2
Questions for understanding: Write your answers below.

1. What lesson does this fable teach about the mule carrying the money?

_____

_____

_____

_____

2. What does this fable say about the character of the robbers?

_____

_____

_____

_____

Lesson 54 The Shepherd Boy and the Wolf

Day 1
Read the fable below. Then fill in the blanks on the next page.

A shepherd boy, ____1____ watched a flock of sheep near a ____2____, got bored sitting all alone on the ____3____. Seeking some company, he called "Wolf! Wolf!" ____4____ loud as he could. This cry brought ____5____ the villagers, and when his neighbors came ____6____ help him, the shepherd boy thought it ____7____ a great joke and laughed at them ____8____ their pains. The shepherd boy continued to summon the villagers whenever he became bored.

The wolf, however, did truly ____9____ at last. The shepherd boy, now really ____10____, shouted in terror: "Pray, do come and help ____11____! The wolf is killing the sheep!"

But ____12____ one paid any attention to his cries. ____13____ one came to his assistance. The wolf ____14____ no cause for fear, and took his ____15____ to bite or kill the whole flock.

No ____16____ believes a liar, even when he speaks the truth.

_____

Day 2
Interesting and curious words

1.   Read the fable, and write the meaning of each word below.

  a. bored _____

  b. assistance _____

  c. summon _ _____

2.   Check your answers in the answer key on p.194. Use a dictionary to find other meanings for the words.

3.   Below, write a sentence using each word as it is used in the fable.

  a. _____

  _____

  b. _____

  _____

  c. _____

  _____

Lesson 54 The Shepherd Boy and the Wolf

Day 1
Fill in the blanks Write your answers below

1. _____   9. _____

2. _____   10. _____

3. _____   11. _____

4. _____   12. _____

5. _____   13. _____

6. _____   14. _____

7. _____   15. _____

8. _____   16. _____

Correct exact words   _____

Correct appropriate words   _____

Total correct words   _____

Day 2
Questions for understanding: Write your answers below.

1. What does this fable tell you about the shepherd boy?

_____

_____

_____

_____

2. What did you learn about often raising an alarm?

_____

_____

_____

_____

117

Lesson 55 The Wolf and the Lamb

Day 1
Read the fable below. Then fill in the blanks on the next page.

A wolf, meeting ____1____ lamb straying from the fold, resolved not ____2____ lay violent hands on him, but to ____3____ some argument to justify to the lamb ____4____ wolf's right to eat him. The wolf said ____5____ the lamb: "Sir, last year you grossly ____6____ me." "Indeed," bleated the lamb in a mournful ____7____ of voice, "I was not even born ____8____ year."

Then said the wolf, "You feed ____9____ my pasture." "No, good sir," replied the ____10____, "I have not yet tasted grass."

Again ____11____ wolf said, "You drink from my well." "____12____," exclaimed the lamb, "I never yet drank ____13____, for as yet my mother's milk is ____14____ food and drink to me."

Upon which the ____15____ seized him and ate him up, saying, "Well! I ____16____ remain supperless, even though you refute every one of my imputations."

The tyrant will always find a pretext for his tyranny.

_____

Day 2
Interesting and curious words

1.   Read the fable, and write the meaning of each word below.

a. pretext _____

b. imputations _____

c. refute _____

2.   Check your answers in the answer key on p. 194. Use a dictionary to find other meanings for the words.

3.   Below, write a sentence using each word as it is used in the fable.

a. _____

_____

b. _____

_____

c. _____

_____

Day 1
Fill in the blanks Write your answers below

1. _____   9. _____

2. _____   10. _____

3. _____   11. _____

4. _____   12. _____

5. _____   13. _____

6. _____   14. _____

7. _____   15. _____

8. _____   16. _____

Correct exact words   _____

Correct appropriate words   _____

Total correct words   _____

Day 2
Questions for understanding: Write your answers below.

1. What do you think of the wolf's arguments?

_____

_____

_____

_____

2. What does this fable teach about evil?

_____

_____

_____

_____

Lesson 56 The Donkey and His Shadow

Day 1
Read the fable below. Then fill in the blanks on the next page.

A traveler hired a ____1____ with a donkey to carry his luggage ____2____ a distant place. The sun was shining in ____3____ strength. The day was intensely hot, and ____4____ traveler stopped to rest. He sought shelter ____5____ the heat under the shadow of the ____6____. As this shadow could give protection ____7____ only one person, the traveler and the owner of ____8____ donkey both claimed it.

A violent dispute arose ____9____ them as to who had the right ____10____ the shadow. The owner maintained that he ____11____ rented the donkey only, and not his ____12____. The traveler asserted that he had, with ____13____ hire of the ass, also hired his ____14____. The quarrel proceeded from words to blows, ____15____ while the men fought, the donkey galloped ____16____ with the luggage.

In quarreling about the shadow, we often lose the substance.

_____

Day 2
Interesting and curious words

1.   Read the fable, and write the meaning of each word below.

a. asserted _____

b. dispute _____

c. maintained _____

2.   Check your answers in the answer key on p.194. Use a dictionary to find other meanings for the words.

3.   Below, write a sentence using each word as it is used in the fable.

a. _____

_____

b. _____

_____

c. _____

_____

120

Lesson 56 The Donkey and His Shadow

Day 1
Fill in the blanks Write your answers below

1. _____   9. _____
2. _____   10. _____
3. _____   11. _____
4. _____   12. _____
5. _____   13. _____
6. _____   14. _____
7. _____   15. _____
8. _____   16. _____

Correct exact words   _____
Correct appropriate words   _____
Total correct words   _____

Day 2
Questions for understanding: Write your answers below.

1. Who should have sat in the shade, and why?

_____

_____

_____

_____

2. What did you learn about arguments from this fable?

_____

_____

_____

_____

Lesson 57 The Peacock and Juno

Day 1
Read the fable below. Then fill in the blanks on the next page.

The peacock complained ___1___ Juno that, while the nightingale pleased everyone's ___2___ with his song, he, the beautiful peacock, ___3___ such a horrid voice that no sooner did ___4___ open his mouth than he became a laughingstock ___5___ all who heard him.

The goddess, to ___6___ him, said: "But you far excel in ___7___ and in size. The splendor of the emerald ___8___ in your neck and you unfold a ___9___ gorgeous with painted plumage."

"But for what purpose have I,"___10___ the bird, "this dumb beauty as long ___11___ I am surpassed in song?"

"The lot of ___12___," replied Juno, "has been assigned by the ___13___ of the Fates. To you, beauty; to ___14___ eagle, strength; to the nightingale, song; to the raven, ___15___, and to the crow, unfavorable foretelling ___16___ the future. These are all contented with the endowments allotted to them."

_____

Day 2
Interesting and curious words

1.   Read the fable, and write the meaning of each word below.

  a. horrid_____

  b. plumage _____

  c. endowments _____

2.   Check your answers in the answer key on p.194. Use a dictionary to find other meanings for the words.

3.   Below, write a sentence using each word as it is used in the fable.

  a. _____

  _____

  b. _____

  _____

  c. _____

  _____

Lesson 57 The Peacock and Juno

Day 1
Fill in the blanks Write your answers below

1. _____
2. _____
3. _____
4. _____
5. _____
6. _____
7. _____
8. _____

9. _____
10. _____
11. _____
12. _____
13. _____
14. _____
15. _____
16. _____

Correct exact words   _____
Correct appropriate words   _____
Total correct words   _____

Day 2
Questions for understanding: Write your answers below.

1. Why does the peacock want to sing?

_____

_____

_____

_____

2. What does this fable say about the talents of different people?

_____

_____

_____

_____

Lesson 58 The Farmer and the Stork

Day 1
Read the fable below. Then fill in the blanks on the next page.

A farmer ____1____ nets on his newly sown land and caught ____2____ number of cranes, which came to pick up ____3____ seed. With them he trapped a stork that had ____4____ his leg in the net and was ____5____ beseeching the farmer to spare his life.

`"Pray ____6____ me, Master," he said, "and let me go ____7____ this once. My broken limb should excite your ____8____. Besides, I am no crane. I am a ____9____, a bird of excellent character. See how ____10____ love and slave for my father and mother. ____11____, too, at my feathers—they are not like ____12____ of a crane."

The farmer laughed aloud and ____13____, "It may be all as you say. I know ____14____ this: I have taken you with these ____15____, the cranes, and you must die in their ____16____."

Birds of a feather flock together.

Day 2
Interesting and curious words

1.   Read the fable, and write the meaning of each word below.

a. sown _____

b. spare _____

c. character _____

2.   Check your answers in the answer key on p.194. Use a dictionary to find other meanings for the words.

3.   Below, write a sentence using each word as it is used in the fable.

a. _____

_____

b. _____

_____

c. _____

_____

Lesson 58 The Farmer and the Stork

Day 1
Fill in the blanks Write your answers below

1. _____   9. _____

2. _____   10. _____

3. _____   11. _____

4. _____   12. _____

5. _____   13. _____

6. _____   14. _____

7. _____   15. _____

8. _____   16. _____

Correct exact words   _____
Correct appropriate words   _____
Total correct words   _____

Day 2
Questions for understanding: Write your answers below.

1 Did the farmer do the right thing?

_____

_____

_____

_____

2. What does this fable teach you about your companions?

_____

_____

_____

_____

Lesson 59 The Wolf and the Shepherd

Day 1
Read the fable below. Then fill in the blanks on the next page.

A wolf followed a ___1___ of sheep for a long time and did ___2___ attempt to injure any of them. The shepherd ___3___ first was on his guard against him, as ___4___ enemy, and kept a strict watch over his ___5___. Day after day, the wolf stayed in the company ___6___ the sheep and never made the slightest effort ___7___ seize one of them. The shepherd began to ___8___ upon the wolf as a guardian of his ___9___, rather than a danger to it.

One day, ___10___ the shepherd was called into the city, he ___11___ the sheep entirely in the wolf's charge. The ___12___, now that he had the opportunity, fell ___13___ the sheep and destroyed the greater part ___14___ the flock. When the shepherd returned to ___15___ his flock destroyed, he exclaimed: "It serves ___16___ right. Why did I trust my sheep to a wolf?"

Day 2
Interesting and curious words

1. Read the fable, and write the meaning of each word below.

   a. seize _____

   b. guardian _____

   c. charge _____

2. Check your answers in the answer key on p.194. Use a dictionary to find other meanings for the words.

3. Below, write a sentence using each word as it is used in the fable.

   a. _____

   _____

   b. _____

   _____

   c. _____

   _____

126

Lesson 59 The Wolf and the Shepherd

Day 1
Fill in the blanks Write your answers below

1. _____
2. _____
3. _____
4. _____
5. _____
6. _____
7. _____
8. _____

9. _____
10. _____
11. _____
12. _____
13. _____
14. _____
15. _____
16. _____

Correct exact words   _____
Correct appropriate words   _____
Total correct words   _____

Day 2
Questions for understanding: Write your answers below.

1. Why did the shepherd not see the true nature of the wolf?

_____

_____

_____

_____

2. What does this fable tell you about familiar things?

_____

_____

_____

_____

Lesson 60 The Milk Woman and Her Pail

Day 1
Read the fable below. Then fill in the blanks on the next page.

A farmer's daughter ____1____ carrying her pail of milk from the ____2____ to the farmhouse, when she began daydreaming. "The ____3____ from selling this milk will buy at least ____4____ hundred eggs. The eggs, allowing for all mishaps, ____5____ produce two hundred and fifty chickens. The chickens ____6____ be ready for market when the poultry ____7____ will be the highest, so by the end of the ____8____, I shall have money enough to buy a ____9____ gown.

In this dress I will go to the Christmas ____10____, where all the young fellows will propose ____11____ me. But I will toss my head and ____12____ them every one." At the same time she ____13____ her head in unison with her thoughts, The ____14____ pail fell to the ground, spilling all ____15____ milk. All her imaginary schemes perished in a ____16____.

When you dream, never lose sight of reality.

_____

Day 2
Interesting and curious words

1.   Read the fable, and write the meaning of each word below.

a. daydreaming _____

b. mishaps _____

c. perished _____

2.   Check your answers in the answer key on p.194. Use a dictionary to find other meanings for the words.

3.   Below, write a sentence using each word as it is used in the fable.

a. _____

_____

b. _____

_____

c. _____

_____

Lesson 60 The Milk Woman and Her Pail

Day 1
Fill in the blanks Write your answers below

1. _____   9. _____

2. _____   10. _____

3. _____   11. _____

4. _____   12. _____

5. _____   13. _____

6. _____   14. _____

7. _____   15. _____

8. _____   16. _____

Correct exact words   _____
Correct appropriate words   _____
Total correct words   _____

Day 2
Questions for understanding: Write your answers below.

1. Why would the farmer's daughter want to reject the young fellows at the party?

_____

_____

_____

_____

2. What does this fable teach you about daydreaming?

_____

_____

_____

_____

Lesson 61 The Tortoise and the Eagle

Day 1
Read the fable below. Then fill in the blanks on the next page.

A tortoise, lazily basking ____1____ the sun, complained to the seabirds of her ____2____ fate: "No one will ever teach me to ____3____ up in the sky like you do." An ____4____, hovering nearby, heard her lamentation and demanded what ____5____ she would give him if he would take ____6____ aloft and float her in the air. "I will ____7____ you," she said, "all the riches of the Red ____8____."

"I will teach you to fly then," said ____9____ eagle. The eagle took the tortoise up in his talons. ____10____ carried her almost to the clouds. Suddenly the ____11____ let her go. She fell on a lofty ____12____, dashing her shell to pieces.

The tortoise exclaimed ____13____ the moment of death: "I have deserved my ____14____ fate, for what had I to do with ____15____ and clouds, who can only with difficulty move ____16____ on the earth?"

If men had all they wished, they would often be ruined.

Day 2
Interesting and curious words

1.   Read the fable, and write the meaning of each word below.

  a. lamentation _____

  b. basking _____

  c. talons _____

2.   Check your answers in the answer key on p.195. Use a dictionary to find other meanings for the words.

3.   Below, write a sentence using each word as it is used in the fable.

  a. _____

  _____

  b. _____

  _____

  c. _____

  _____

Lesson 61 The Tortoise and the Eagle

Day 1
Fill in the blanks Write your answers below

1. _____

2. _____

3. _____

4. _____

5. _____

6. _____

7. _____

8. _____

9. _____

10. _____

11. _____

12. _____

13. _____

14. _____

15. _____

16. _____

Correct exact words   _____

Correct appropriate words   _____

Total correct words   _____

Day 2
Questions for understanding: Write your answers below.

1. Why did the eagle let go of the turtle?

_____

_____

_____

_____

2. What does this fable say about people's wishes?

_____

_____

_____

_____

Lesson 62 The Dog, the Cock, and the Fox

Day 1
Read the fable below. Then fill in the blanks on the next page.

A dog and a cock, ____1____ great friends, agreed to travel together. ____2____ nightfall they took shelter in a thick wood. The ____3____, flying up, perched himself on the branches of ____4____ tree, while the dog found a bed below ____5____ the hollow trunk. When the morning dawned, the ____6____, as usual, crowed very loudly several times.

A fox ____7____ the sound and, wishing to make a breakfast ____8____ him, came and stood under the branches, saying, "____9____ I would love to make the acquaintance of ____10____ owner of so magnificent a voice."

The cock, ____11____ his civilities, said: "Sir, I wish you would ____12____ me the favor of going around to the ____13____ trunk below me and waking my porter, so ____14____ may open the door and let you in." ____15____ the fox approached the tree, the dog sprang ____16____ and caught him, and tore him to pieces.

_____

Day 2
Interesting and curious words

1.   Read the fable, and write the meaning of each word below.

   a. magnificent _____

   b. civilities _____

   c. porter _____

2.   Check your answers in the answer key on p.195. Use a dictionary to find other meanings for the words.

3.   Below, write a sentence using each word as it is used in the fable.

   a. _____

   _____

   b. _____

   _____

   c. _____

   _____

Lesson 62 The Dog, the Cock, and the Fox

Day 1
Fill in the blanks Write your answers below

1. _____   9. _____

2. _____   10. _____

3. _____   11. _____

4. _____   12. _____

5. _____   13. _____

6. _____   14. _____

7. _____   15. _____

8. _____   16. _____

Correct exact words _____

Correct appropriate words _____

Total correct words _____

Day 2

Questions for understanding: Write your answers below.

1. What was the fox's mistake?

_____

_____

_____

_____

2. What does this fable teach you?

_____

_____

_____

_____

Lesson 63 The Eagle and the Jackdaw

Day 1
Read the fable below. Then fill in the blanks on the next page.

An eagle, flying ____1____ from his perch on a lofty rock, seized ____2____ a lamb and carried him aloft in his ____3____. A jackdaw, who witnessed the capture of the ____4____, was stirred with envy and determined to emulate ____5____ strength and flight of the eagle. He flew ____6____ with a great whir of his wings and ____7____ upon a large ram, with the intention of ____8____ him off. Instead, his claws became entangled in ____9____ ram's fleece. Although he fluttered with his feathers ____10____ much as he could, he was not able ____11____ release himself.

The shepherd, seeing what had happened, ____12____ up and caught the bird. He immediately clipped the ____13____ wings, took him home that night, and gave ____14____ to his children.

"Father, what kind of bird is ____15____?" He replied, "To my certain knowledge he is a jackdaw, but he ____16____ like you to think he is an eagle."

Use your own skills; do not attempt to emulate those of others

---

Day 2
Interesting and curious words

1. Read the fable, and write the meaning of each word below.

a. stirred _____

b. emulate _____

c. entangled _____

2. Check your answers in the answer key on p.195. Use a dictionary to find other meanings for the words.

3. Below, write a sentence using each word as it is used in the fable.

a. _____

_____

b. _____

_____

c. _____

_____

134

Lesson 63 The Eagle and the Jackdaw

Day 1

Fill in the blanks Write your answers below

1. _____   9. _____

2. _____   10. _____

3. _____   11. _____

4. _____   12. _____

5. _____   13. _____

6. _____   14. _____

7. _____   15. _____

8. _____   16. _____

Correct exact words   _____

Correct appropriate words _____

Total correct words   _____

Day 2

Questions for understanding: Write your answers below.

1. Why did the jackdaw become entangled in the sheep's wool?

_____

_____

_____

_____

2. What was the jackdaw's mistake?

_____

_____

_____

_____

Lesson 64 The Grasshopper and the Owl

Day 1
Read the fable below. Then fill in the blanks on the next page.

An owl, accustomed ____1____ feed at night and to sleep during the ____2____, was greatly disturbed by the noise of a ____3____. The owl earnestly asked her to stop chirping. ____4____ grasshopper refused to stop. The more the owl ____5____, the louder and louder the grasshopper chirped. When ____6____ owl saw that she could get no redress and that ____7____ words were despised, the owl approached the chatterer ____8____ a stratagem.

"Since I cannot sleep," she said, "____9____ of your song (which, believe me, is sweet as ____10____ lyre of Apollo), I shall indulge myself in ____11____ some nectar that the god Pallas, gave me. ____12____ you think you will like it, come to ____13____ and we will drink it together."

The grasshopper, ____14____ was thirsty, and pleased with the praise of her ____15____, eagerly flew up. The owl came forth from her hollow, ____16____ her, and put her to death.

Day 2
Interesting and curious words

1.   Read the fable, and write the meaning of each word below.

   a. redress _____

   b. nectar _____

   c. indulge _____

2.   Check your answers in the answer key on p.195. Use a dictionary to find other meanings for the words.

3.   Below, write a sentence using each word as it is used in the fable.

   a. _____

   _____

   b. _____

   _____

   c. _____

   _____

Lesson 64 The Grasshopper and the Owl

Day 1
Fill in the blanks Write your answers below

1. _____   9. _____

2. _____   10. _____

3. _____   11. _____

4. _____   12. _____

5. _____   13. _____

6. _____   14. _____

7. _____   15. _____

8. _____   16. _____

Correct exact words   _____
Correct appropriate words   _____
Total correct words   _____

Day 2
Questions for understanding: Write your answers below.

1. Why did the owl invite the grasshopper to share the nectar?

_____

_____

_____

_____

2. What does this fable tell you about continually annoying someone?

_____

_____

_____

_____

Lesson 65 The Two Soldiers and the Robber

Day 1
Read the fable below. Then fill in the blanks on the next page.

Two soldiers, Hans and Gustaf, _____1_____ together, were set upon by a robber. ____2____
fled, while Gustaf stood his ground and ____3____ himself with his stout right hand. The
robber ____4____ slain.

The timid Hans ran up and drew ____5____ sword. Then, throwing back his traveling cloak, he
____6____, "I'll at him, and I'll take care he ____7____ learn whom he has attacked."

On this, Gustaf, ____8____ had fought with the robber, answered, "I only ____9____ that you
had helped me just now, even ____10____ it had been only with those words, for
____11____ would have been the more encouraged, believing them ____12____ be true. But
now, put up your sword ____13____ its sheath and hold your equally useless tongue,
____14____ you can deceive others who do not know ____15____. I, who have experienced
what speed you run away, know ____16____ that no one can depend on your valor."

_____

Day 2
Interesting and curious words

1.   Read the fable, and write the meaning of each word below.

   a. stout _____

   b. valor _____

   c. sheath _____

2. Check your answers in the answer key on p.195. Use a dictionary to find other meanings for
   the words.

3. Below, write a sentence using each word as it is used in the fable.

a. _____

   _____

b. _____

   _____

c. _____

   _____

Lesson 65 The Two Soldiers and the Robber

Day 1
Fill in the blanks Write your answers below

1. _____   9. _____

2. _____   10. _____

3. _____   11. _____

4. _____   12. _____

5. _____   13. _____

6. _____   14. _____

7. _____   15. _____

8. _____   16. _____

Correct exact words   _____
Correct appropriate words   _____
Total correct words   _____

Day 2
Questions for understanding: Write your answers below.

1. Why did Hans draw his sword?

_____

_____

_____

_____

2. What kind of person was the soldier Hans?

_____

_____

_____

_____

Lesson 66 The Stag at the Pool

Day 1
Read the fable below. Then fill in the blanks on the next page.

A stag, overpowered ____1____ heat, came to a spring to drink. When ____2____ saw his own shadow reflected in the water, ____3____ greatly admired the size and variety of his ____4____, but felt angry with himself for having such ____5____ and weak feet. While he was contemplating himself, ____6____ lion appeared at the pool and crouched to ____7____ upon him. The stag immediately took to flight ____8____ ran as fast as he could. As long ____9____ the ground was smooth and open, he kept himself ____10____ at a safe distance from the lion.

But when ____11____ entered the woods, he became entangled by his ____12____. The lion quickly came up to him and ____13____ him. When too late, the stag reproached himself: "Woe ____14____ me! How I have deceived myself! These feet, ____15____ would have saved me, I despised, and I gloried ____16____ these antlers, which have proved my destruction."

What is most truly valuable is often underrated.

Day 2
Interesting and curious words

1.   Read the fable, and write the meaning of each word below.

   a. contemplating _____

   b. crouched _____

   c. gloried _____

2.   Check your answers in the answer key on p.195. Use a dictionary to find other meanings for the words.

3.   Below, write a sentence using each word as it is used in the fable.

   a. _____

   _____

   b. _____

   _____

   c. _____

   _____

Lesson 66 The Stag at the Pool

Day 1
Fill in the blanks Write your answers below

1. _____   9. _____

2. _____   10. _____

3. _____   11. _____

4. _____   12. _____

5. _____   13. _____

6. _____   14. _____

7. _____   15. _____

8. _____   16. _____

Correct exact words   _____
Correct appropriate words   _____
Total correct words   _____

_____

Day 2
Questions for understanding: Write your answers below.

1. Why did the stag think his antlers were better than his feet?

_____

_____

_____

2. What does this fable tell you about personal beauty?

_____

_____

_____

_____

Lesson 67 The Lion and the Shepherd

Day 1
Read the fable below. Then fill in the blanks on the next page.

A lion, roaming _____1_____ a forest, stepped upon a thorn. Soon afterward _____2_____ came up to a shepherd and fawned upon _____3_____, wagging his tail as if to say, "I _____4_____ a supplicant and seek your aid." The shepherd _____5_____ examined the beast, discovered the thorn, and placing _____6_____ paw upon his lap, pulled out the thorn. Thus _____7_____ of his pain, the lion returned into the_____8_____.Sometime after, the shepherd, being imprisoned on _____9_____ false accusation, was condemned "to be cast to _____10_____ lions" as the punishment for his imputed crime. _____11_____ when the lion was released from his cage, _____12_____ recognized the shepherd as the man who had healed him. _____13_____ of attacking him, he approached and placed his foot upon the shepherd's _____14_____. The king, as soon as he heard the tale, _____15_____ ordered the lion to be set free again in the forest, and the _____16_____ to be pardoned and restored to his friends.

Day 2
Interesting and curious words

1.   Read the fable, and write the meaning of each word below.

   a. fawned _____

   b. supplicant _____

   c. condemned _____

2.   Check your answers in the answer key on p.195. Use a dictionary to find other meanings for the words.

3.   Below, write a sentence using each word as it is used in the fable.

   a. _____

   _____

   b. _____

   _____

   c. _____

   _____

Lesson 67 The Lion and the Shepherd

Day 1
Fill in the blanks Write your answers below

1. _____

2. _____

3. _____

4. _____

5. _____

6. _____

7. _____

8. _____

9. _____

10. _____

11. _____

12. _____

13. _____

14. _____

15. _____

16. _____

Correct exact words   _____

Correct appropriate words   _____

Total correct words   _____

Day 2
Questions for understanding: Write your answers below.

1. What does this story tell you about the character of the shepherd?

_____

_____

_____

_____

2. Why would the king pardon the shepherd and the lion?

_____

_____

_____

_____

Lesson 68 The Seaside Travelers

Day 1
Read the fable below. Then fill in the blanks on the next page.

Some travelers, ____1____ on a desert island, were walking along the ____2____. They climbed to the summit of a tall cliff ____3____, looking over the sea, saw in the distance what they ____4____ was a large ship: "Oh look, there is a ____5____ come to rescue us."

They waited in the hope ____6____ seeing it enter the harbor. But the object ____7____ smaller as it was driven nearer to shore ____8____ the wind: "It is not a ship. It looks like a ____9____ boat. Perhaps some of us can use it to get ____10____ the island and find someone to rescue the rest of us."

____11____, however, it reached the beach, they discovered that ____12____ was only a large bundle of sticks, and ____13____ of them said to his companions: "We have waited ____14____ no reason. After all there is nothing to ____15____ but a load of wood."

Our mere anticipations ____16____ life outrun its realities.

_____

Day 2
Interesting and curious words

1.   Read the fable, and write the meaning of each word below.

   a. summit _____

   b. rescue _____

   c. anticipations_ _____

2.   Check your answers in the answer key on p.195. Use a dictionary to find other meanings for the words.

3.   Below, write a sentence using each word as it is used in the fable.

   a. _____

   _____

   b. _____

   _____

   c. _____

   _____

Lesson 68 The Seaside Travelers

Day 1

Fill in the blanks Write your answers below

1. _____
2. _____
3. _____
4. _____
5. _____
6. _____
7. _____
8. _____

9. _____
10. _____
11. _____
12. _____
13. _____
14. _____
15. _____
16. _____

Correct exact words   _____
Correct appropriate words   _____
Total correct words   _____

Day 2

Questions for understanding: Write your answers below.

1. What does this fable tell you about wishes and reality?

_____

_____

_____

_____

2. What might the travelers have done instead of watching the bundle of sticks?

_____

_____

_____

_____

Lesson 69 The Lion and the Dolphin

Day 1
Read the fable below. Then fill in the blanks on the next page.

A ___1___, roaming by the seashore, saw a dolphin lift up ___2___ head out of the waves, and suggested that they ___3___ an alliance, saying that of all the animals they ___4___ to be the best friends, since the one was ___5___ king of beasts on the earth, and the other ___6___ the sovereign ruler of all the inhabitants of the ___7___. The dolphin gladly consented to this request.

Not long ___8___ the lion had a combat with a wild bull, ___9___ called on the dolphin to help him. The dolphin, ___10___ quite willing to give him assistance, was unable to do so, ___11___ he could not by any means reach the land. ___12___ lion abused him as a traitor.

The dolphin replied, "___13___, my friend, blame not me, but nature, which, while ___14___ me the sovereignty of the sea, has quite denied ___15___ the power of living upon the land."

Know your ___16___ skills and those of your friends.

___

Day 2
Interesting and curious words

1.   Read the fable, and write the meaning of each word below.

   a. contract _____

   b. alliance _____

   c. abused_____

2.   Check your answers in the answer key on p.195. Use a dictionary to find other meanings for the words.

3.   Below, write a sentence using each word as it is used in the fable.

   a. _____

   _____

   b. _____

   _____

   c. _____

   _____

Lesson 69 The Lion and the Dolphin

Day 1

Fill in the blanks Write your answers below

1. _____   9. _____

2. _____   10. _____

3. _____   11. _____

4. _____   12. _____

5. _____   13. _____

6. _____   14. _____

7. _____   15. _____

8. _____   16. _____

Correct exact words   _____
Correct appropriate words   _____
Total correct words   _____

Day 2

Questions for understanding: Write your answers below.

1. How does this alliance make sense?

_____

_____

_____

_____

2. What does this fable teach you about different talents?

_____

_____

_____

_____

Lesson 70 The Lion, the Fox, and the Donkey

Day 1
Read the fable below. Then fill in the blanks on the next page.

The lion, ____1____ fox, and the donkey entered into an agreement to ____2____ each other
in the chase. Having secured a ____3____ booty, the lion on their return from the forest
____4____ the donkey to divide the booty into the due ____5____ for each of the three partners
in the treaty. ____6____ donkey carefully divided the spoil into three equal shares
____7____ modestly requested the two others to make the first ____8____.
The lion burst into a great rage, and ____9____ the donkey Then he asked the fox to
do ____10____ the favor to make a division. The fox accumulated ____11____ that they had
killed into one large heap and ____12____ to himself the smallest possible morsel.

The lion said, "____13____ has taught you, my very excellent fellow, the art
____14____ division? You are perfect to a fraction."
"I learned ____15____ from the donkey," replied the fox, "by witnessing his fate."

Happy is the ____16____ who learns from the misfortunes of others.

Day 2
Interesting and curious words

1.   Read the fable, and write the meaning of each word below.

  a. booty _____

  b. devoured _____

  c. morsel _____

2.   Check your answers in the answer key on p.195. Use a dictionary to find other meanings
        for the words.

3.   Below, write a sentence using each word as it is used in the fable.

  a. _____

  _____

  b. _____

  _____

  c. _____

  _____

Lesson 70 The Lion, the Fox, and the Donkey

Day 1

Fill in the blanks Write your answers below

1. _____

2. _____

3. _____

4. _____

5. _____

6. _____

7. _____

8. _____

9. _____

10. _____

11. _____

12. _____

13. _____

14. _____

15. _____

16. _____

Correct exact words _____

Correct appropriate words _____

Total correct words _____

Day 2

Questions for understanding: Write your answers below.

1. What kind of person is the lion?

_____

_____

_____

_____

2. What does this fable teach you about dealing with power?

_____

_____

_____

_____

Lesson 71 The Miser

Day 1
Read the fable below. Then fill in the blanks on the next page.

A miser ____1____ all that he had and bought a lump of ____2____. He buried his gold in a hole in the ground ____3____ the side of an old wall. He went to ____4____ at it every day. One of his workmen observed his ____5____ visits to the spot and decided to watch his ____6____. The workman soon discovered the secret of the hidden treasure, ____7____ digging down, came to the lump of gold and ____8____ it.

The miser, on his next visit, found the hole ____9____ and began to tear his hair and to cry ____10____. A neighbor, seeing him overcome with grief and learning ____11____ cause, said, "Pray do not grieve so, but go ____12____ take a stone, place it in the hole, and ____13____ that the gold is still lying there. The stone ____14____ just as valuable as the gold, for when the ____15____ was there, you really didn't have it, as you ____16____ not make the slightest use of it."

Day 2
Interesting and curious words

1.   Read the fable, and write the meaning of each word below.

   a. lump _____

   b. grieve _____

   c. overcome _____

2.   Check your answers in the answer key on p.195. Use a dictionary to find other meanings for the words.

3.   Below, write a sentence using each word as it is used in the fable.

   a. _____

   _____

   b. _____

   _____

   c. _____

   _____

Lesson 71 The Miser

Day 1
Fill in the blanks Write your answers below

1. _____
2. _____
3. _____
4. _____
5. _____
6. _____
7. _____
8. _____

9. _____
10. _____
11. _____
12. _____
13. _____
14. _____
15. _____
16. _____

Correct exact words   _____
Correct appropriate words   _____
Total correct words   _____

Day 2
Questions for understanding: Write your answers below.

1. What kind of person is the miser?

_____
_____
_____
_____

2. What does this fable tell you about the value of gold or jewels?

_____
_____
_____
_____

Lesson 72 The Ants and the Grasshopper

Day 1
Read the fable below. Then fill in the blanks on the next page.

All summer ____1____ the grasshopper sat in the shade, played his fiddle, ____2____ sang songs. The ants spent the summer working hard ____3____ the hot sun to store grain for winter.

"Ho, ____4____. Why do you work in the hot sun? The ____5____ is nice. You should take time to play. It is ____6____ more fun in the shade."

"We have to get ____7____ for winter when there is cold and snow, Mr.____8____ . We have no time for play."

The ants were spending a ____9____ winter's day drying grain collected in the summertime. The ____10____, perishing with famine, passed by and earnestly begged for ____11____ little food. "Why did you not store up food ____12____ the summer?" asked the ants.

"I spent the summer ____13____ fun and singing. I had no time for collecting ____14____ when the weather was so wonderful," he replied. "If ____15____ were foolish enough to sing and have fun all the ____16____, and do no work, you can't expect us to share our hard work in the winter."

_____

Day 2
Interesting and curious words

1. Read the fable, and write the meaning of each word below.

   a. fiddle _____

   b. perishing _____

   c. famine _____

2. Check your answers in the answer key on p.195. Use a dictionary to find other meanings for the words.

3. Below, write a sentence using each word as it is used in the fable.

   a. _____

   _____

   b. _____

   _____

   c. _____

   _____

Lesson 72 The Ants and the Grasshopper

Day 1

Fill in the blanks Write your answers below

1. _____   9. _____

2. _____   10. _____

3. _____   11. _____

4. _____   12. _____

5. _____   13. _____

6. _____   14. _____

7. _____   15. _____

8. _____   16. _____

Correct exact words   _____
Correct appropriate words   _____
Total correct words   _____

Day 2

Questions for understanding: Write your answers below.

1. What does this fable tell you about work and play?

_____

_____

_____

_____

2. What do you think about what the ants did?

_____

_____

_____

_____

Lesson 73 The Donkey and the Grasshoppers

Day 1
Read the fable below. Then fill in the blanks on the next page.

A donkey ____1____ walking through a field one day. He heard some ____2____ chirping. The donkey was delighted with the sound. He ____3____ to be able to sing like the grasshoppers. "Grasshoppers," ____4____ said, "You have such beautiful voices. What do you ____5____ to make them so melodious?" "Chirp, chirp. We eat ____6____ the dew," they replied.

"That is easy," said the ____7____. "I will eat only dew and have a beautiful ____8____ too." The donkey decided that he would live ____9____ on dew. He would eat no grass. So the donkey ____10____ up before the sun every day. He licked the ____11____ from all the plants in the field. After the sun came ____12____ and the dew went away, the donkey practiced singing. He ____13____ and practiced. No matter how much he practiced singing, ____14____ always sounded like "Hee haw."

The donkey ate no grass. ____15____ got thinner and thinner, and in a short time he ____16____ of hunger.

What is good for one may be bad for another.

Day 2
Interesting and curious words

1. Read the fable, and write the meaning of each word below.

   a. delighted _____

   b. melodious _____

   c. dew _____

2. Check your answers in the answer key on p.196. Use a dictionary to find other meanings for the words.

3. Below, write a sentence using each word as it is used in the fable.

   a. _____

   _____

   b. _____

   _____

   c. _____

   _____

Lesson 73 The Donkey and the Grasshopper

Day 1

Fill in the blanks Write your answers below

1. _____
2. _____
3. _____
4. _____
5. _____
6. _____
7. _____
8. _____

9. _____
10. _____
11. _____
12. _____
13. _____
14. _____
15. _____
16. _____

Correct exact words   _____
Correct appropriate words   _____
Total correct words   _____

Day 2

Questions for understanding: Write your answers below.

1. What does this fable say about imitating others?

_____

_____

_____

_____

2. What does this fable tell you about the donkey?

_____

_____

_____

_____

Lesson 74 The Donkey and His Masters

Day 1
Read the fable below. Then fill in the blanks on the next page.

A donkey belonged ____1____ an herb seller who gave him too little ____2____ and too much work. The donkey made a petition to Jupiter to ____3____ from his present service and be given to another ____4____ .

"You may be very sorry you made such a ____5____ ,"Jupiter, warned him. Jupiter caused the donkey to be ____6____ to a tile maker. Shortly afterward, finding that he ____7____ heavier loads to carry and harder work in the brick field, he petitioned for ____8____ change of master.

Jupiter told him that this would ____9____ the last time that he could grant his request. ____10____ ordained that the donkey be sold to a tanner. ____11____ donkey found that he had fallen into worse ____12____ . Noting his new master's occupation, he groaned: "It ____13____ have been better for me either to be starved ____14____ the one or to be overworked by the other ____15____ my former masters, than to have been bought by my present ____16____ , who will, even after I am dead, tan my hide and make me useful to him."

Day 2
Interesting and curious words

1.   Read the fable, and write the meaning of each word below.

 a. petition _____

 b. service _____

 c. ordained_____

2.   Check your answers in the answer key on p.196. Use a dictionary to find other meanings for the words.

3.   Below, write a sentence using each word as it is used in the fable.

 a. _____

 _____

 b. _____

 _____

 c. _____

 _____

Lesson 74 The Donkey and His Masters

Day 1
Fill in the blanks Write your answers below

1. _____   9. _____

2. _____   10. _____

3. _____   11. _____

4. _____   12. _____

5. _____   13. _____

6. _____   14. _____

7. _____   15. _____

8. _____   16. _____

Correct exact words   _____
Correct appropriate words   _____
Total correct words   _____

Day 2
Questions for understanding: Write your answers below.

1. What kind of person is the donkey?

_____

_____

_____

_____

2. What does this fable tell you about making changes in your life?

_____

_____

_____

_____

Lesson 75 The Hen and the Golden Eggs

Day 1
Read the fable below. Then fill in the blanks on the next page.

One day a farmer was ___1___ home from market. He saw a little hen high in a ___2___.
"Save me! Save me!" cried the little hen." The fox ___3___ after me."

The farmer tucked the little hen under his ___4___ and took her to his cottage. "Look wife," said
he, "___5___ the pretty little hen I've got." "What a fine ___6___ she will make," exclaimed the
wife.

"No, Please don't eat ___7___. I will lay an egg for you every day," said the hen. So the
___8___ day the little hen laid a little egg of ___9___. The little hen laid a golden
egg every day after that. The ___9___ and his wife supposed that the little hen must contain
a ___11___ lump of gold in its inside.

"If we kill the little hen, ___12___ will get all the gold at once," they thought. Having
___13___ so, they found to their surprise that the little hen ___14___ in no respect from any
other hen. The foolish ___15___, hoping to become rich all at once, deprived themselves of the
___16___ of which they were assured day by day.

Day 2
Interesting and curious words

1.   Read the fable, and write the meaning of each word below.

    a. supposed _____

    b. respect _____

    c. exclaimed _____

2.   Check your answers in the answer key on p.196. Use a dictionary to find other meanings
        for the words.

3.   Below, write a sentence using each word as it is used in the fable.

    a. _____

    _____

    b. _____

    _____

    c. _____

    _____

Lesson 75 The Hen and the Golden Eggs

Day 1

Fill in the blanks Write your answers below

1. _____
2. _____
3. _____
4. _____
5. _____
6. _____
7. _____
8. _____

9. _____
10. _____
11. _____
12. _____
13. _____
14. _____
15. _____
16. _____

Correct exact words   _____
Correct appropriate words   _____
Total correct words   _____

Day 2

Questions for understanding: Write your answers below.

1. What motivated the wife to kill the little hen?

_____

_____

_____

_____

2. What does this fable teach you about patience?

_____

_____

_____

_____

Lesson 76 The Lion and the Mouse

Day 1
Read the fable below. Then fill in the blanks on the next page.

A great lion _____1_____ awakened from sleep by a mouse running over his face. _____2_____up angrily, he caught the little mouse and was _____3_____ to kill him, when the mouse piteously pleaded, saying, "If _____4_____ will only spare my life, I will be sure to repay _____5_____ kindness."

The lion laughed "What can a tiny mouse ever _____6_____ to help a great lion?" The lion thought this was so _____7_____ that he let the little mouse go.

Not long after this, _____8_____ lion was caught by some hunters. They tied him _____9_____ the ground by strong ropes. The mouse heard his roar. The _____10_____ crawled up to the lion during the dark of _____11_____. He gnawed the lion's ropes with his teeth and _____12_____ him free, exclaiming: "You laughed at the idea that _____13_____ could ever be able to help you, You released _____14_____, not expecting any repayment of your favor. Now you _____15_____ that even a little mouse to can help a great _____16_____."

_____

Day 2
Interesting and curious words

1.   Read the fable, and write the meaning of each word below.

   a. piteously _____

   b. gnawed _____

   c. pleaded _____

2.   Check your answers in the answer key on p.196. Use a dictionary to find other meanings for the words.

3.   Below, write a sentence using each word as it is used in the fable.

   a. _____

   _____

   b. _____

   _____

   c. _____

   _____

160

Lesson 76 The Lion and the Mouse

Day 1

Fill in the blanks Write your answers below

1. _____

2. _____

3. _____

4. _____

5. _____

6. _____

7. _____

8. _____

9. _____

10. _____

11. _____

12. _____

13. _____

14. _____

15. _____

16. _____

Correct exact words   _____

Correct appropriate words   _____

Total correct words   _____

Day 2

Questions for understanding: Write your answers below.

1. What was the lion thinking when he let the mouse go?

_____

_____

_____

_____

2. What does this fable teach you about kindness?

_____

_____

_____

_____

Lesson 77 The Lion and the Boar

Day 1
Read the fable below. Then fill in the blanks on the next page.

One ___1___ day, the sun was broiling hot. The earth was ___2___, and most of the water holes had dried up. ___3___ the beasts were thirsty and looking for water. A ___4___ and a boar came at the same moment to a ___5___ well to drink. They fiercely disputed which of them should ___6___ first.

"I got here first," said the boar. "I should be ___7___ first to drink." "I should drink first," said the lion. "___8___ the king of the beasts!"

The lion and the ___9___ began to fight. The fight got fiercer and fiercer. ___10___ the lion and the boar were engaged a mortal ___11___. They stopped for a moment to catch their breath ___12___ an even fiercer renewal of the fight. While they ___13___ resting, they saw some vultures waiting in the ___14___ to feast on the one that should fall first.

They made up their ___15___ at once and went together to drink at the well , saying: "It is better for us to make friends, than to become the ___16___ of crows or vultures."

_____

Day 2
Interesting and curious words

1.   Read the fable, and write the meaning of each word below.

 a. fiercer _____

 b. mortal _____

 c. engaged _____

2.   Check your answers in the answer key on p.196. Use a dictionary to find other meanings for the words.

3.   Below, write a sentence using each word as it is used in the fable.

 a. _____

 _____

 b. _____

 _____

 c. _____

 _____

162

Lesson 77 The Lion and the Boar

Day 1

Fill in the blanks Write your answers below

1. _____

2. _____

3. _____

4. _____

5. _____

6. _____

7. _____

8. _____

9. _____

10. _____

11. _____

12. _____

13. _____

14. _____

15. _____

16. _____

Correct exact words   _____

Correct appropriate words   _____

Total correct words   _____

Day 2

Questions for understanding: Write your answers below.

1. Why did the lion and the boar fight?

_____

_____

_____

_____

2.. What lesson did the boar and the lion learn?

_____

_____

_____

_____

Lesson 78 The Eagle and the Hawk

Day 1
Read the fable below. Then fill in the blanks on the next page.

An eagle, overwhelmed ____1____ sorrow, sat upon the branches of a tree in company with a ____2____. "Why," said the hawk, "do I see you with ____3____ a rueful look?"

"I seek," the eagle replied, "a mate suitable for ____4____, and I am not able to find one." "Take me," ____5____ the hawk. "I am much stronger than you are."

"Why, ____6____ you able to secure a living by your plunder?" asked the eagle. "Well, ____7____ have often caught and carried away an ostrich in my ____8____," answered the hawk.

The eagle, persuaded by these words, accepted him as her ____9____. Shortly after the nuptials, the eagle said, "Fly off and ____10____ me back the ostrich you promised me." The hawk, soaring aloft ____11____ the air, brought back the shabbiest possible mouse, stinking ____12____ the length of time it had lain about the ____13____.

"Is this," asked the eagle, "the faithful fulfillment of ____14____ promise to me?" The hawk replied, "That I might ____15____ your royal hand, there is nothing that I would not have ____16____, however much I knew that I must fail in the performance."

Day 2
Interesting and curious words

1.   Read the fable, and write the meaning of each word below.

   a. nuptials _____

   b. rueful _____

   c. plunder _____

2.   Check your answers in the answer key on p.196. Use a dictionary to find other meanings for the words.

3.   Below, write a sentence using each word as it is used in the fable.

   a. _____

   _____

   b. _____

   _____

   c. _____

   _____

Lesson 78 The Eagle and the Hawk

Day 1

Fill in the blanks Write your answers below

1. _____

2. _____

3. _____

4. _____

5. _____

6. _____

7. _____

8. _____

9. _____

10. _____

11. _____

12. _____

13. _____

14. _____

15. _____

16. _____

Correct exact words   _____

Correct appropriate words _____

Total correct words   _____

Day 2

Questions for understanding: Write your answers below.

1. What caused the eagle to marry the hawk?

_____

_____

_____

_____

2. What kind of person is the hawk in this fable?

_____

_____

_____

_____

Lesson 79 The Kingdom of the Lion

Day 1
Read the fable below. Then fill in the blanks on the next page.

The beasts of the ____1____ and forest had a lion as their king. He ____2____ the nicest king there ever was. He was never ____3____, wrathful, cruel, or tyrannical. The lion was just as ____4____ and gentle as a king could be. By royal proclamation he ____5____ together an assembly of all the birds and beasts. The ____6____ king issued a plan for a universal league for peace ____7____ the animals

"My loyal subjects," he said, "I hereby proclaim ____8____ universal peace among all animals. The wolf will be ____9____ with the lamb; the cat will be friends with ____10____ rat; the panther will be friends with the kid; the ____11____ will be friends with the stag; and the dog will ____12____ friends with the rabbit. All animals shall live together ___13___ peace and harmony."

The rabbit said, "Oh, how I ____14____ longed to see this day in which the ____15____ shall take their place as equals by the side of the strong." Having had his say, the ____16____ ran for his life.

The pleasing words of many a politician may not be realistic.

Day 2
Interesting and curious words

1. Read the fable, and write the meaning of each word below.

 a. wrathful _____

 b. league _____

 c. harmony _____

2. Check your answers in the answer key on p.196. Use a dictionary to find other meanings for
     the words.

3. Below, write a sentence using each word as it is used in the fable.

 a.

 _____

 _____

 b. _____

 _____

 c. _____

 _____

166

Lesson 79 The Kingdom of the Lion

Day 1

Fill in the blanks Write your answers below

1. _____   9. _____

2. _____   10. _____

3. _____   11. _____

4. _____   12. _____

5. _____   13. _____

6. _____   14. _____

7. _____   15. _____

8. _____   16. _____

Correct exact words   _____

Correct appropriate words _____

Total correct words   _____

Day 2

Questions for understanding: Write your answers below.

1. Why did the rabbit run?

_____

_____

_____

_____

2. What does the rabbit's action tell you about the lion's proclamation?

_____

_____

_____

_____

Lesson 80 Hercules and the Farmer

Day 1
Read the fable below. Then fill in the blanks on the next page.

A farmer was ____1____ a wagonload of turnips to market along a muddy ____2____ lane. He came to a deep muddy rut. The wheels ____3____ his wagon sank down deep. The rustic farmer, stupefied and aghast, ____4____ looking at the wagon sunk so deep in the mud. He ____5____ know what to do, so he did nothing. "Oh, woe is ____6____. I cannot get my turnips to market," he cried. "My ____7____ is deep in the mud."

After a time he uttered loud ____8____ to Hercules to come and help him: "Oh, Hercules! My ____9____ is stuck in the rut. I cannot get my ____10____ to market. You are the strongest man in ____11____ world. Pick up my wagon and carry it out of the ____12____ so I can get my turnips to the market."

Hercules ____13____ to the farmer and said: "Put your shoulders to the ____14____, my man. Goad on your oxen. Never call upon ____15____ to do your work for you until you have tried ____16____ best to help yourself, or you will ask in vain."

Self-help is the best help.

_____

Day 2
Interesting and curious words

1.   Read the fable, and write the meaning of each word below.

   a. aghast _____

   b. goad _____

   c. uttered _____

2.   Check your answers in the answer key on p.196. Use a dictionary to find other meanings
      for the words.

3.   Below, write a sentence using each word as it is used in the fable.

   a. _____

   _____

   b. _____

   _____

   c. _____

   _____

Lesson 80 Hercules and the Farmer

Day 1
Fill in the blanks Write your answers below

1. _____   9. _____

2. _____   10. _____

3. _____   11. _____

4. _____   12. _____

5. _____   13. _____

6. _____   14. _____

7. _____   15. _____

8. _____   16. _____

Correct exact words   _____
Correct appropriate words   _____
Total correct words   _____

Day 2
Questions for understanding: Write your answers below.

1. What kind of person was the farmer in this fable?

_____

_____

_____

_____

2. What does this fable teach you about overcoming your problems?

_____

_____

_____

_____

Professor Bloomer's AESOP'S FABLES

Answer key

Day - 1

Cloze Exact Word Answers

Professor Bloomer's Aesop's Fables

Answer key: Day 1

Fill in the Blanks 1-8

1. The Fox and the Mask	2. The Fox and the Grapes	3. The Fox and the Leopard	4. The Boy Bathing
1. the	1. ripe	1. about	1. in
2. all	2. She	2. two	2. He
3. an	3. them	3. various	3. help
4. placed	4. not	4. fox	4. hand
5. a	5. away	5. more	5. the
6. value	6. are	6. am	6. the
		7. Beauty	7. me

5. The Rabbit and the Hound	6. The Dog in the Manger	7. The Donkey and His Driver	8. The Hawk, the Eagle, and the Pigeons
1. rabbit	1. in	1. driven	1. by
2. gave	2. time	2. and	2. called
3. him	3. oxen	3. deep	3. at
4. is	4. placed	4. of	4. into
5. hound	5. one	5. by	5. made
6. between	6. eat	6. When	6. of
7. dinner	7. allow	7. man	7. could
	8. helps	8. own	8. a

Professor Bloomer's Aesop's Fables

Answer key: Day 1

Fill in the Blanks (Continued) 9 - 16

9. The Wolf and the Lion	10. The Thrush and the Fowler	11. The Dog and the Oyster	12. The Wolf, the Fox, and the Ape
1. a	1. was	1. to	1. fox
2. lair	2. not	2. his	2, the
3. and	3, so	3. down	3. between
4. Standing	4, long	4. be	4. case
5. You	5. and	5. in	5. not
6. To	6. point	6. this	6. claim
7. righteously	7. I	7. everything	7. stolen
	8. pleasant	8. often	8. if
	9. life		

13. The Partridge and the Fowler	14. The Dolphins, the Whales, and the Herring	15. The Dog's House	16. The Cock and the Jewel
1. caught	1. waged	1. the	1. was
2. him	2. the	2. small	2. himself
3. his	3. lifted	3. cold	3. jewel
4. live	4. said	4. However	4. found
5. you	5. they	5. asleep	5. be
6. The	6. of	6. to	6. My
7. life	7. be	7. Now	7. jewels
8. to	8. than	8. an	8. corn
9. your	9. in	9. himself	9. Each

Professor Bloomer's Aesop's Fables

Answer key: Day 1

Fill in the Blanks (continued) 17 - 24

17. The Flies and the Honey Pot	18. The Gnat and the Bull	19. The Mother Dog and Her Whelps	20. The Fox and the Lion
1. were	1. on	1. ready	1. who
2. had	2. there	2. a	2. one
3. in	3. about	3. When	3. the
4. smeared	4. noise	4. to	4. nearly
5. use	5. would	5. The	5. the
6. and	6. I	6. mother	6. but
7. they	7. shall	7. whelps	7. first
8. the	8. are	8. able	8. was
9. destroyed	9. than	9. to	9. up
		10. shepherd	10. with

21. The Flea and the Man	22. The Donkey and the Charger	23. The Camel	24. The Monkeys and Their Mother
1. with	1. of	1. saw	1. is
2. said	2. and	2. was	2. each
3. on	3. had	3. he	3. it
4. much	4. to	4. camel	4. the
5. Oh	5. heavily	5. and	5. It
6. destroy	6. him	6. courage	6. loved
7. much	7. of	7. seeing	7. of
8. will	8. dead	8. became	8. his
9, no	9. these	9. his	9. one
10. should	10. charger	10. him	10. often

Professor Bloomer's Aesop's Fables

Answer key: Day 1

Fill in the Blanks (continued) 25 - 32

25. The Boy and the Filberts	26. The Peacock and the Crane	27. The Wolf and the Lion	28. The Wolf and the Horse
1. hand	1. its	1. at	1. coming
2. grasped	2. by	2. become	2. a
3. but	3. saying	3. to	3. advise
4. hand	4. gold	4. I	4. is
5. the	5. the	5. acre	5. a
6. his	6. bit	6. of	6. for
7. hand	7. crane	7. of	7. eating
8. his	8. heaven	8. indulging	8. the
9. satisfied	9. stars	9. upon	9. my
10. easily	10. a	10. a	10. People
	11. Fine	11. of	11. good

29. The Master and His Dogs	30. The Donkey and the Old Shepherd	31. The Thief and the Housedog	32. The Horse and the Donkey
1. was	1. his	1. in	1. of
2, great	2. shepherd	2. He	2. a
3. and	3. approaching	3. in	3. heavily
4. alive	4. let	4. he	4. I
5. to	5. will	5. As	5. heels
6. seeing	6. donkey	6. meat	6. his
7. It	7. you	7. little	7. to
8. for	8. double	8. alert	8. after
9. oxen	9. shepherd	9. This	9. sent
10. we	10. I	10. make	10. donkey
11. not	11. matter	11. these	11. him
12. his	12. change	12. make	12. your
	13. but	13. some	13. condition

Professor Bloomer's Aesop's Fables

Answer key: Day 1

Fill in the Blanks (continued) 33 - 40

33. The Old Man and Death	34. The Widow and the Sheep	35. The Crow and the Pitcher	36. The Hawk and the Nightingale
1. man	1. had	1. crow	1. high
2. forest	2. to	2. and	2. beautiful
3. for	3. she	3. with	3. hawk
4. his	4. so	4. to	4. down
5. and	5. the	5. water	5. lose
6. am	6. Why	6. it	6. go
7. come	7. weight	7. to	7. satisfy
8. his	8. If	8. in	8. food
9. it	9. butcher	9. stones	9. hawk
10, man	10. but	10. and	10. lost
11. lift	11. there	11. pitcher	11. food
12. upon	12. not	12. reach	12. of
13. may	13. always	13. the	13. within

37. The Monkey and the Camel	38. The Spendthrift and the Swallow	39. The Kid and the Wolf	40. The Boasting Traveler
1. the	1. young	1. without	1. had
2. the	2. all	2. a	2. when
3. dancing	3. left	3. turned	3. told
4. amidst	4. swallow	4. that	4. he
5. the	5. The	5. I	5. had
6. to	6. gaily	6. favor	6. was
7. himself	7. come	7. I	7. that
8. turn	8. many	8. while	8. near
9. moved	9. renewed	9. dancing	9. me
10. that	10. unfortunate	10. and	10. as
11. beat	11. unhappy	11. said	11. saying
12. out	12, before	12. I	12. true
13. It	13. yourself	13. have	13. this

176

Professor Bloomer's Aesop's Fables

Answer key: Day 1

Fill in the Blanks (continued) 41 - 48

41. The Trees and the Axe	42. The Two Travelers and the Axe	43. The Man and His Two Sweethearts	44. The Weasel and the Mice
1. came	1. were	1. hair	1. getting
2. to	2. an	2. women	2. to
3. The	3. said	3. was	3. did
4. him	4. friend	4. years	4. down
5. the	5. but	5. by	5. A
6. axe	6. not	6. whenever	6. upon
7. to	7. of	7. some	7. to
8. strokes	8. who	8. on	8. manner
9. old	9. have	9. wife	9. after
10. of	10. to	10. in	10. escaped
11. The	11. you	11. Thus	11. a
12. we	12. you	12. both	12. weasel
13. ash	13. not	13. not	13. succeed
14. lives	14. who	14. who	14. really

45. The Mischievous Dog	46. The Rabbits and the Frogs	47. The Ant and the Dove	48. The Crow and the Raven
1. young	1. by	1. went	1. was
2. to	2. the	2. its	2. considered
3. bite	3. They	3. being	3. always
4. around	4. their	4. stream	4. by
5. people	5. into	5. drowning	5. the
6. dog	6. off	6. hanging	6. Seeing
7. and	7. resolve	7. let	7. into
8. proudly	8. the	8. her	8. of
9. day	9. and	9. safely	9. could
10. do	10. safety	10. came	10. wondered
11. That	11. frogs	11. his	11. The
12. order	12. his	12. the	12. us
13. of	13. as	13. the	13. it
14. all	14. there	14. bird catcher	14. crow
15. dog	15. than	15. noise	15. omen

Professor Bloomer's Aesop's Fables

Answer key: Day 1

Fill in the Blanks (continued) 49 - 56

49. The North Wind and the Sun	50. The Fox and the Crow	51. The Donkey and His Purchaser	52. The Peasant and the Apple Tree
1. and	1. having	1. wished	1. had
2. the	2. a	2. its	2. bore
3. who	3. A	3. animal	3. for
4. his	4, meat	4. donkey	4. cut
5. North	5. How	5. with	5. hands
6. with	6. the	6. all	6. The
7. blasts	7. fairness	7. the	7. down
8. around	8. were	8. greatest	8. spare
9. of	9. be	9. man	9. lighten
10. to	10. said	10. him	10. them
11. suddenly	11. the	11. how	11. a
12. traveler	12. a	12. him	12. reached
13. he	13. fox	13. I	13. a
14. at	14. the	14. that	14. honey
15. bathed	15. enough	15. the	15. on
			16. of

53. The Mules and the Robbers	54. The Shepherd Boy and the Wolf	55. The Wolf and the Lamb	56. The Donkey and His Shadow
1. with	1. who	1. a	1. man
2. filled	2. village	2. to	2. to
3. mule	3. hillside	3. find	3. full
4. as	4. as	4. the	4. the
5. burden	5. out	5. to	5. from
6. bells	6. to	6. insulted	6. donkey
7. with	7. was	7. tone	7. for
8. sudden	8. for	8. last	8. the
9. places	9. come	9. in	9. between
10. the	10. alarmed	10, lamb	10. to
11. sword	11. me	11. the	11. had
12. no	12. no	12. No	12. shadow
13. had	13. No	13. water	13. the
14. The	14. had	14. both	14. shadow
15. that	15. time	15. wolf	15. and
16. lost	16. one	16. won't	16. off

Professor Bloomer's Aesop's Fables

Fill in the Blanks (continued) 57 - 64

57. The Peacock and Juno	58. The Farmer and the Stork	59. The Wolf and the Shepherd	60. The Milk Woman and Her Pail
1. to	1. placed	1. flock	1. was
2. ear	2. a	2. not	2. field
3. had	3. his	3. at	3. money
4. he	4. fractured	4. an	4. three
5. to	5. earnestly	5. movements	5. will
6. console	6. save	6. of	6. will
7. beauty	7. free	7. to	7. price
8. shines	8. pity	8. look	8. year
9. tail	9. stork	9. flock	9. new
10. said	10. I	10. when	10. parties
11. as	11. Look	11. left	11. to
12. each	12. those	12. wolf	12. refuse
13. will	13. said	13. upon	13. tossed
14. the	14. only	14. of	14. milk
15. favorable	15. robbers	15. find	15. the
16. of	16. company	16. me	16. second

61. The Tortoise and the Eagle	62. The Dog, the Cock, and the Fox	63. The Eagle and the Jackdaw	64. The Grasshopper and the Owl
1. in	1. being	1. down	1. to
2. hard	2. At	2. upon	2. day
3. fly	3. cock	3. talons	3. grasshopper
4. eagle	4. a	4. lamb	4. The
5. reward	5. in	5. the	5. begged
6. her	6. cock	6. around	6. the
7. give	7. heard	7. settled	7. her
8. Sea	8. of	8. carrying	8. by
9. the	9. How	9. the	9. because
10. He	10. the	10. as	10. the
11. eagle	11, suspecting	11. to	11. drinking
12. mountain	12. do	12. ran	12. If
13. in	13. hollow	13. jackdaw's	13. me
14. present	14. he	14. him	14. who
15. wings	15. When	15. it	15. voice
16. about	16. out	16. would	16. seized

Professor Bloomer's Aesop's Fables

Answer key: Day 1

Fill in the Blanks (continued) 65 - 72

65. The Two Soldiers and the Robber	66. The Stag at the Pool	67. The Lion and the Shepherd	68. The Seaside Travelers
1. traveling	1. by	1. through	1. lost
2. Hans	2. he	2. he	2. seashore
3. defended	3. he	3. him	3. and
4. was	4. horns	4. am	4. thought
5. his	5. slender	5. boldly	5. ship
6. said	6. a	6. his	6. of
7. shall	7. spring	7. relieved	7. looked
8. who	8. and	8. forest	8. by
9. wish	9. as	9. a	9. small
10. if	10. easily	10. the	10. off
11. I	11. he	11. But	11. When
12. to	12. horns	12. he	12. it
13. in	13. caught	13. Instead	13. one
14. until	14. is	14. lap	14. for
15. you	15. which	15. instead	15. see
16. well	16. in	16. shepherd	16. of

69. The Lion and the Dolphin	70. The Lion, the Fox, and the Donkey	71. The Miser	72. The Ants and the Grasshopper
1. lion	1. the	1. sold	1. long
2. its	2. help	2. gold	2. and
3. contract	3. large	3. by	3. in
4. ought	4. asked	4. look	4. Ants
5. the	5. portion	5. frequent	5. weather
6. was	6. The	6. movements	6. much
7. ocean	7. and	7. and	7. ready
8. after	8. choice	8. stole	8. Grasshopper
9. and	9. devoured	9. empty	9. fine
10. though	10. him	10. aloud	10. grasshopper
11. as	11. all	11. the	11. a
12. The	12. left	12. and	12. during
13. No	13. Who	13. pretend	13, having
14. giving	14. of	14. is	14. food
15. me	15. it	15. gold	15. you
16. own	16. person	16. did	16. summer

Professor Bloomer's Aesop's Fables

Fill in the Blanks (continued) 73 - 80

73. The Donkey and the Grasshopper	74. The Donkey and His Masters	75. The Hen and the Golden Eggs	76. The Lion and the Mouse
1. was	1. to	1. walking	1. was
2. grasshoppers	2. food	2. tree	2. Rising
3. wanted	3. change	3. is	3. about
4. he	4. master	4. coat	4. you
5. eat	5. request	5. see	5. your
6. only	6. sold	6. dinner	6. do
7. donkey	7. had	7. me	7. funny
8. voice	8. another	8. next	8. the
9. only	9. be	9. gold	9. to
10. got	10. He	10. farmer	10. mouse
11. dew	11. The	11. great	11. night
12. up	12. hands	12. we	12. set
13. practiced	13. would	13. done	13. I
14. it	14. by	14. differed	14. me
15. He	15. of	15. pair	15. know
16. died	16. owner	16. gain	16. lion

77. The Lion and the Boar	78. The Eagle and the Hawk	79. The Kingdom of the Lion	80. Hercules and the Farmer
1. summer	1. with	1. field	1. driving
2. baked	2. hawk	2. was	2. country
3. All	3. such	3. mean	3. of
4. lion	4. me	4. kind	4. stood
5. small	5. returned	5. called	5. didn't
6. drink	6. are	6. lion	6. me
7. the	7. I	7. among	7. wagon
8. I'm	8. talons	8. a	8. cries
9. boar	9. mate	9. friends	9. wagon
10. Soon	10. bring	10. the	10. turnips
11. combat	11. into	11. tiger	11. the
12. for	12. from	12. be	12. mud
13. were	13. fields	13. in	13. came
14. distance	14. your	14. have	14. wheels
15. quarrel	15. attain	15. weak	15. others
16. food	16. promised	16. rabbit	16. your

Professor Bloomer's
AESOP'S FABLES

Answer key

Day - 2

Interesting and Curious Words

Professor Bloomer's Aesop's Fables

Answer key: Day 2

Interesting and Curious Words 1 - 12

1. The Fox and the Mask	2. The Fox and the Grapes	3. The Fox and the Leopard	4. The Boy Bathing
1. rummage: search	1. famished: very hungry	1. exhibited: showed or displayed	1. unconcernedly: disinterestedly or indifferently
2. admirable: highly regarded	2. trellised: held off the ground by an interwoven structure	2. decorated: beautify, or adorned	2. scold: blame, berate, yell at
	3. vain: unsuccessful or futile		3. imprudence: carelessness or recklessness

5. The Rabbit and the Hound	6. The Dog in the Manger	7. The Donkey and His Driver	8. The Hawk, the Eagle, and the Pigeons
1. lair: home or den	1. prevented: stopped	1. bolted: ran	1. cote: shelter for pigeons
2. mocked: teased	2. manger: bin for animal feed	2. precipice: cliff	2. consented: agreed
		4. endeavoring: trying	3. havoc: chaos or disturbance

9. The Wolf and the Lion	10. The Thrush and the Fowler	11. The Dog and the Oyster	12. The Wolf, The Fox, and the Ape
1. seizing: grabbing	1. cast: threw	1. folly: foolishness	1. adjudge: determine, settle
2. jeer: taunt, scoff	2. deprived: taken away	2. utmost: greatest	2. stoutly: strongly
3. righteous: moral, honest, ethical	3. fowler: person who kills or captures birds	3. relish: enjoyment, delight	3. undertook: agreed to do something

Professor Bloomer's Aesop's Fables

Answer key: Day 2

Interesting and Curious Words (continued) 13 - 24

13. The Partridge and the Fowler 1. beseeched: begged 2. enticed: tempted 3. scruple: doubt, hesitation	**14. The Dolphins, the Whales, and the Herring** 1. umpire: referee, judge 2. affairs: business, activities	**15. The Dog's House** 1. determined: decided 2. accommodate: adjust, make room for	**16. The Cock and the Jewel** 1. precious: very valuable 2. 2. exclaimed: spoke or cried out loudly and suddenly
17. The Flies and the Honey Pot 1. greedily: hungrily 2. smeared: spread 3. expiring: dying	**18. The Gnat and the Bull** 1. inquired: asked 2. gnat: small bug	**19. The Mother Dog and Her Whelps** 1. whelp: give birth To puppies 2. litter: group of baby animals	**20. The Fox and the Lion** 1. alarmed: frightened 2. commenced: began
21. The Flea and the Man 1. annoyed: irritated 2. tolerated: allowed	**22. The Donkey and the Charger** 1. charger: war horse 2. ungrudgingly: without resentment 3. 3. commiserate: express sympathy	**23. The Camel** 1. looming: appearing in a threatening way 2. 2. vast: huge 3. meekness: timidity	**24. The Monkeys and their Mother** 1. smothered: overwhelmed or suppressed 2. nurtured: encouraged, cared for

Professor Bloomer's Aesop's Fables

Answer key: Day 2

Interesting and Curious Words (continued) 25 - 36

25. The Boy and the Filberts 1. bystander: onlooker 2. bitterly: resentfully 3. lamented: complained	**26. The Peacock and the Crane** 1. gorgeous: beautiful 2. ridiculing: mocking, teasing 3. soar: glide high in the air	**27. The Wolf and the Lion** 1. wretched: miserable 2. immense: huge 3. repentance: regret	**28. The Wolf and the Horse** 1. addressed: direct attention to 2. advised: recommended 3. indulged: given enjoyment to
29. The Master and His Dogs 1. spare: keep from harm 2. mistreat: abuse 3. yoke: frame for harnessing animals to something they pull	**30. The Donkey and the Old Shepherd** 1. appeal: plead 2. alarm: distress 3. rejoined: answered	**31. The Thief and the Housedog** 1. pacify: calm 2. alert: warn 3. beware: be careful	**32. The Horse and the Donkey** 1. peace: silence 2. derided: ridiculed 3. trappings: ornaments, accessories
33. The Old Man and Death 1. wearied: tired 2. summons: call 3. wayside: side of a road	**34. The Widow and the Sheep** 1. solitary: single, alone 2. fleece: wool 3. shearing: cutting wool from a sheep	**35. The Crow and the Pitcher** 1. delight: joy 2. grief: sorrow 3. invention: creation, discovery	**36. The Hawk and the Nightingale** 1. swooped: swept down 2. satisfy: fulfill 3. pursuing: chasing

Professor Bloomer's Aesop's Fables

Interesting and Curious Words (continued) 37 - 48

37. The Monkey and the Camel	38. The Spendthrift and the Swallow	39. The Kid and the Wolf	40. The Boasting Traveler
1. divert: draw attention from 2. utterly: completely 3. indignation: anger, outrage	1. spendthrift: person who is wasteful, extravagant 2. wrought: made 3. twittering: chirping, tweeting	1. prey: victim, animal eaten as food 2. favor: grant a wish 3. complied: fulfilled a wish	1. heroic: brave 2. leapt: jumped 3. witness: observer

41. The Trees and the Axe	42. The Two Travelers and the Axe	43. The Man and His Two Sweethearts	44. The Weasel and the Mice
1. felled: cut down 2. lamenting: expressing regret 3. retained: saved	1. journeying: traveling 2. mode: manner	1. courted: dated, wooed 2. advanced: far along 3. zealous: enthusiastic	1. supposing: assuming 2. snare: noose or trap 3. crafty: tricky, sneaky

45. The Mischievous Dog	46. The Rabbits and the Frogs	47. The Ant and the Dove	48. The Crow and the Raven
1. merit: value 2. distinction: importance 3. notoriety: dishonor	1. timidity: fearfulness 2. perpetual: continuous 3. 3. scampered: ran quickly	1. quench: satisfy 2. plucked: pulled off 3. design: plan	1. omen: sign of the future, prediction 2. forebode: predict evil

Professor Bloomer's Aesop's Fables

Answer key: Day 2

Interesting and Curious Words (continued) 49-60

49. The North Wind and the Sun	50. The Fox and the Crow	51. The Donkey and His Purchaser	52. The Peasant and the Apple Tree
1. wayfaring: traveling 2. genial: friendly mild 3. keener: stronger, colder and more penetrating	1. stratagem: clever plan 2. refute: prove false 3. wit: intelligence	1. idle: lazy 2. halter: rope or leather device for leading animals	1. harbor: safe place 2. entreated: begged 3. resolved: decided

53. The Mules and the Robbers	54. The Shepherd Boy and the Wolf	55. The Wolf and the Lamb	56. The Donkey and His Shadow
1. panniers: large baskets 2. scuffle: fight 3. bewailed: expressed misery	1. bored: tired of something that is not interesting 2. assistance: help 3. summon: call	1. pretext: excuse 2. imputations: accusations 3. refute: prove false	1. asserted: stated strongly 2. dispute: argument 3. maintained: stated

57. The Peacock and Juno	58. The Farmer and the Stork	59. The Wolf and the Shepherd	60. The Milk Woman and Her Pail
1. horrid: terrible 2. plumage: feathers 3. endowments: abilities or talents	1. sown: planted 2. spare: save 3. character: integrity, personal qualities	1. seize: grab, hold 2. guardian: protector 3. charge: care, responsibility	1. daydreaming: imagining 2. mishaps: accidents 3. perished: died

Professor Bloomer's Aesop's Fables

Answer key: Day 2

Interesting and Curious Words (continued) 61 - 72

61. The Tortoise and the Eagle	62. The Dog, the Cock, and the Fox	63. The Eagle and the Jackdaw	64. The Grasshopper and the Owl
1. lamentation: expression of grief	1. magnificent: great, wonderful	1. stirred: motivated	1. redress: remedy
2. basking: lying in warmth	2. civilities: polite actions	2. emulate: copy	2. nectar: sweet juice
3. talons: claws	3. porter: doorkeeper	3. entangled: caught, tangled	3. Indulge: yield to desire

65. The Soldiers and the Robber	66. The Stag at the Pool	67. The Lion and the Shepherd	68. The Seaside travelers
1 stout: strong	1. contemplating: thinking about	1. fawned: flattered	1. summit: peak
2. valor: bravery	2. crouched: bent in preparation to pounce	2. supplicant: a person who pleads or begs	2. rescue: save, release
3. sheath: sword cover	3. gloried: felt pride in	3. condemned: judged and sentenced to punishment	3. anticipations: expectations

69. The Lion and the Dolphin	70. The Lion, the Fox, and the Donkey	71. The Miser	72. The Ants and the Grasshopper
1. contract: agree	1. booty: loot	1. lump: shapeless mass	1. fiddle: violin
2. alliance: cooperative association	2. devoured: ate	2. grieve: mourn	2. perishing: dying
3. abused: insulted	3. morsel: small piece	2. overcome: overwhelmed	3. famine: starvation

Professor Bloomer's Aesop's Fables

Answer key: Day 2

Interesting and Curious Words (continued) 73 - 80

73. The Donkey and the Grasshopper	74. The Donkey and His Masters	75. The Hen and the Golden Eggs	76. The Lion And The Mouse
1. delighted: highly pleased 2. melodious: musical 3. dew: water droplets on cool outdoor surfaces	1. petition: request 2. service: job 3. ordained: commanded	1. supposed: thought 2. respect: condition, trait 3. exclaimed: spoke or cried out loudly and suddenly	1. piteously: pathetically 2. gnawed: chewed 3. pleaded: begged

77. The Lion and the Boar	78. The Eagle and the Hawk	79. The Kingdom of the Lion	80. Hercules and the Farmer
1. fiercer: more violent 2. mortal: deadly 3. engaged: involved	1. nuptials: wedding ceremony 2. rueful: full of regret or sorrow 3. plunder: loot	1. wrathful: angry 2. league: association 3. harmony: friendly agreement	1. aghast: shocked 2. goad: prod 3. uttered: spoke

EPILOGUE

Dr Bloomer's Aesop's Fables for Reading Comprehension.

The Aesop's Fables are essentially moral folk tales handed down over the centuries. When authors are known, they usually hark back to ancient Greek and Roman times. Most of the available English translations of Aesop's fables occurred during the nineteenth century. The nineteenth century translators tended to take pride in the nuances of the English language. Our current American English is much simplified from the ornate Victorian language style of these translators. Many words common during that language expansionist time have drifted into obscurity. Other words have been deemed offensive during our current politically correct times.

There once was, a person called Aesop who was credited short pithy statements demarking some moral percept. As best we can determine Aesop was born a slave in about 620 BCE. He was owned by several masters and was finally freed by his master Jadmon, who gave him his liberty as a reward for his learning and wit.. Aesop is remembered as a great teacher, a moralist, a censor of vice, and a supporter of virtue.

We can look upon Aesop's fables as a style of writing or a brand name much the name Kleenix is used for any facial tissue or Xerox is used for all copiers regardless of manufacture. So to the label ,Aesop's Fable, is used for writings by anybody in ancient times who wrote in the fable form. Many of the fables credited to Aesop were written by others many years after his death in the fable style

In essence Aesop is credited with invention the fable form as a style for teaching moral and social behavior. Thus the term Aesop's fables are a collection of moral stories by various authors over a span of hundreds of years, all written in the fable style of Aesop

The term Aesop's Fable is stylstic and contains several elements according to Townsend (1879):

1. A Fable is instructive and seeks to foster some moral maxim, social duty, or political truth.

2, A true Fable, describes human behavior. It aims at the representation of human motive, and the improvement of human conduct,

3. A fable uses animal characters and conceals its design under the guise of fictitious characters, by giving speech to the animals, the birds, the trees, or the beasts.

4. The character of each beast is consistent: The FOX should be always cunning, the HARE (RABBIT) timid, the LION bold, the WOLF cruel, the BULL strong, the HORSE proud, the ASS (DONKEY) patient, the SERPENT (SNAKE) sneaky, the JACKDAW impulsive, and the OWL wise. People are usually Farmers, Hunters, Robbers, or Tradesmen and often hot too bright.

5. A fable is short and clearly makes it's point.

6. A fable leads the reader, unconsciously toward behavior that is pure, honorable, and praiseworthy, and teacher the reader to be alert to deceit

7. A fable excites the reader's indignation against what is low, ignoble, unworthy; and the truth that deeds of wrong will not pass unpunished.

Many of these fables are characterized by the strictest observance of these rules. They are occupied with one short narrative, from which the moral naturally flows, and with which it is intimately associated.

I have had to slightly modify this nineteenth century language for modern readers. I have been careful not to over simplify the vocabulary of these fables to the level of language compression common in modern elementary school texts. I, like my forebearers, believe in language expansion. Youth must be exposed to vocabulary to understand it. If you do not understand a word, you cannot use it in thinking. A limited vocabulary produces gaps in the ability to think. Simple words make simple minds.

I have tried to keep each fable true to it's original meaning. While some of these ancient morals maybe offensive to some in our age of politically correct denial, they are part of the mature of mankind and are better dealt with to prepare children for their futures than not.

The underlying theme of Aesop's fables is that we each have certain skills and talents as epitomized by the character of each of the animals. The fables demonstrate that each of us should become aware of out own nature and when we emulate that of another disruption occurs.

A second underlying common theme has to do with awareness of trickery by others for their own advantage our reader is admonished to be alert, to control his impulses

Cloze Comprehension Training

Over the years Educators have spent considerable energy trying to find a magic way to enhance children's reading comprehension. The results efforts have largely been neutral. Part of the problem is there is no easy magic way to bend a child's neurons to the task of increased comprehension, only increasing maturity, reading and hard work will succeed. Another part of the problem is the basic neural development of children's brains requires a certain level of maturity. Reading comprehension skills are contingent upon language skills. Comprehension skills are dependent upon the development of functional cognitive processes, that is the brain has to learn to get understanding and inference from language These neurons begin to complete their connections about age nine, approximately fourth grade for most children. Naturally, this maturity is a bit earlier for some and later for others.

While neural maturity is one essential part of reading comprehension, other things like ability to focus on reading material itself, understanding the words, having relevant experiences in memory, and relating the written word to these memories are all necessary components to adequate comprehension.

Some fifty years ago, among the many schemes that Educators have been put forward to enhance reading comprehension was answering pre-questions before reading the paragraph itself. This technique is a direct offshoot of the SQ3R and other comprehension and study methods. With this scheme the appropriate comprehension questions were answered by the reader <u>before</u> reading the paragraph. Then the paragraph was read, followed by the same set of questions. The theory being that the pre-questions would alert the child to look for these important facts and ideas within the reading material.

Back in the late 1950's Andrew Hertzian and I decided to test this pre-question theory. It was just about that time when Harold Taylor published his Cloze Procedure Readability idea. Taylor removed every 10th word from a paragraph and asked readers fill in the blank The more correct fill-ins the more readable, the easier the paragraph, or conversely the better the reader understood it. Taylor named the process after the old Gestalt psychology term Closure which was essentially making a "good" representation from partial stimuli.

Reading difficulty of the prose is just the opposite side of the reading comprehension coin. We decided to include a test of Cloze paragraphs along with regular reading paragraph in our pre-question study. We counterbalanced several paragraphs with Cloze vs. regular reading and both pre-questions and post questions with post questions only. In those days scientific research was more respected in education. Principals and teachers were eager to cooperate. We had no trouble getting access to a number of eighth grade classrooms for our experiment.

When we tallied up the data we received a couple of surprises. First, children who answered the pre-questions whether with Cloze or regular reading were significantly poorer on the *identical* questions after reading the paragraph. Clearly there is something in the Pre-Question technique that inhibits reading comprehension. The Pre-Question learners actually did significantly worse on the exact same questions after reading the paragraph than before reading. The reading the paragraph itself apparently served only to confuse them.

If you just think about this for a minute, Pre-Questions are not such a good idea. What happens in reality is after the pre-questions the child does not have to read every word, but simply skims for keywords to answer questions. Further the material has now lost it's freshness. The learner does not feel the need to focus as hard The learner, by answering the Pre-Questions has reduced the mystery and the intent to learn
The Second, more surprising result was, children with Cloze paragraphs who had ten percent of their reading material deleted, did significantly better on the post questions, in every instance, than those children who had the standard reading paragraphs. Since they had not only to read, but to write the missing words, they paid more attention and focused on the more meaning of the paragraph.

Since reading comprehension improved with Cloze paragraphs, it was only a small step to exploring Cloze as a technique for improving a reader's comprehension. It occurred to me that if Cloze skill really reflected reading ability, perhaps training students to be proficient at Cloze would improve reading ability.

I was teaching a class in reading improvement for college students. I developed a series of 250 word passages at 10 readability levels increasing from pre-primer to grade 6 from five different basal reader series with every tenth word missing. The students did two Cloze lessons each week. If they got 96% or better correct they moved up to the next level of difficulty. Less than 96% correct they remained at the same reading level. When they finished the highest level they didn't have to come to class any more. I gave a standardized reading test at the beginning, and intended to give one at the end. By the end of the semester I had only one student left. Hardly a respectable test of the Cloze procedure. I did have however have the students GPA's. I found the students in my Cloze program increased their own GPA's 1.3 grade levels. From an average of 2.0 to 3.3 The remainder of the University did not show any change in GPA. This was very encouraging.

We did several more tests of this Cloze Comprehension Training. With several types of materials. We found similar GPA results and a significant increases in Iowa Standard Reading Test scores for a university class in reading methods. Similar significant results for Cloze Comprehension Training in a sixth grade class and a college freshmen psychology class. Then we did a large cross-sectional study of students from Grade five to High School seniors. The findings showed significantly greater growth in Reading, Vocabulary, and Language Skills as measured on the Comprehensive Test of Basic Skills. Each time we have used Cloze Comprehension Training it has resulted in increased Standardized teat scores and/or improved school grades

A variant of Cloze Procedure, Multiple Choice Cloze, has been tried by several experimenters. It has been generally unsuccessful. The reason is the multiple choice format with it's several options, does not allow the learner explore his own store of experiences to find an answer. With Cloze procedure the learner is required to think for himself.

Fables are an excellent medium for Cloze Comprehension Training. Given the moral goals of fables, you want the students to think about and develop their own associations to the moral percepts depicted, Cloze which develops increased focus on the content is a natural for increasing the impact of the message inherent in the fable,.

www.ingramcontent.com/pod-product-compliance
Lightning Source LLC
Chambersburg PA
CBHW080934040426
42443CB00015B/3411

9 780984 029518